THE EXPERTS' GUIDE

Kan A. Thomas

Poised Polished Professional

POISED POLISHED PROFESSIONAL
THE EXPERTS' GUIDE TO EXECUTIVE PRESENCE

Copyright © 2018 Karen A. Thomas

All rights reserved. No part of this BOOK may be used or reproduced mechanically, electronically, or by any other means, including photocopying, without prior written consent of the author. It is illegal to copy this post to a website or distribute it by any other means without permission from the Author.

ISBN-13: 978-1718652965

ISBN-10: 1718652968

Published By ICK com. llc Publishing House©
Edited By ICK Publishing & Rachel Crook, SUNY, New Paltz
Cover Design and Book Design By ICK Publishing©

THE EXPERTS' GUIDE TO EXECUTIVE PRESENCE

Poised Polished Professional

Book Dedications

I dedicate this book to an amazing person in my life who; without his constant support, encouragement, and love; this endeavor would not be possible.

To Ken – my amazing husband, biggest cheerleader, chauffeur and builder of confidence. Ken has allowed me to pursue my dream of becoming a recognized etiquette expert in my field through our sharing of ideas, long winded conversations (some at 2 am!), marketing successes and failures, and countless tv, radio and book ventures that we have journeyed through together. He escorts me to most, if not all of my etiquette appearances, business ventures, and college trainings. He does so with a smile, kind word, and of course, full-on networking behind the scenes with clients as I work. May God continue to bless him with good health, patience to put up with me, and the continuous kind heartedness he has gained from his late father – Big Ken. I know he is looking down upon us with a gentle smile and nod of confidence.

~ Karen Thomas

Poised Polished Professional

CONTENTS

Book Dedications..5
Foreword..9
Introduction..13

Chapter I – Executive Presence Defined........................15
   Etiquette & Refinement & Its Role in Executive Presence.................17
   3 Pillars of Executive Presence...19

Chapter II – Pillar 1 - Gravitas......................................21
   Confidence...25
   Decisiveness..30
   Integrity..31
   Emotional Intelligence..33
   Vision...38

Chapter III – Pillar 2 – Communication........................45
   Conversation Etiquette, Cell & Telephone Etiquette.............................47
   Netiquette & Paper Correspondence..60
   Networking Etiquette...70
   Body Language..79
   Dealing with Difficult People..85

Chapter IV – Pillar 3 – Appearance...............................93
   Grooming Posture...95
   Attire Etiquette..109
   First Impression & Reputation Management.....................................117

Chapter V - Attainment & Execution of Executive Presence......125
   Attainment & Execution of Executive Presence.................................127

About the Compiler and Co Author's..............................129
   Karen A. Thomas...131
   Nancy Hoogenboom...135
   Leona Johnson..139
   Danielle Richardson..143
   Carolyn Powery...147

Index..150

Poised Polished Professional

FOREWORD

When I think of POISED, POLISHED, and PROFESSIONAL and Executive Presence I envision many of the past and present business leaders, such as (**Bill Gates**, co-founder of Microsoft, **Warren Buffett**, CEO of Berkshire Hathaway, **Steve Jobs**, CEO of Apple, **Marillyn Hewson** Chairman, President, and CEO, Lockheed Martin, **Sheryl Sandberg** COO, Facebook, **Ginni Rometty** Chairman, President, and CEO, IBM, **Ruth Porat** SVP and CFO, Google, Alphabet and **Condoleezza Rice** founding partner of RiceHadleyGates LLC.) just to name a few. They all lead us with good communication techniques, tone, style, and decorum demonstrating they're all credible professionals with diplomacy.

Today each of us has our own style and personality, not right or wrong, good or bad... It's just the way we are.

Our personalities are often reflected in the way we think and behave. I've read there are four basic normal personality styles. We all have one of them (or maybe a combination of several of them) and the people you work with and live with all have different personality styles. It's so easy to see ourselves meaning our own personal style as being the best one, or the only one, or better yet the normal one. None of these styles is inherently difficult, but they certainly are different. If you stay stuck in thinking that only your style is good or right, you'll automatically have difficulty with 3\4 of the world just because they're different.

I commend Karen A.Thomas and all her Co-authors, Nancy Hoogenboom, Leona Johnson, Danielle Richardson, Carolyn Powery for bringing their teaching essentials into this book guiding all levels with being POISED, POLISHED, and PROFESSIONAL with Executive Presence. I believe its the only way to be.

Irene Prokopiw
CEO and Founder of ICK Com. LLC ICK Publishing
We are Beautiful Magazine©

Poised Polished Professional

THE EXPERTS' GUIDE TO EXECUTIVE PRESENCE

Models Attorney Neal White, Gina White, Actress
Photos courtesy of Teddy

Poised Polished Professional

Introduction

Jumping right into the heart of this book and the reasoning behind its conception, I believed that it was time for two things to happen. One of which was to unite etiquette experts with a book collaboration on our favorite subject: etiquette; and this has been an enlightening experience. The other reason was to assist business professionals in achieving career success by offering a step-by-step guide on how to achieve Executive Presence, and why it has become so prevalent in the business arena.

With this being stated and defined, I feel the need to offer a brief synopsis of how this book will benefit those looking to attain and achieve Executive Presence-- which will be discussed in detail. Each chapter outlined will offer a guideline or a sort of "how to" for execution of this endeavor. Rather than a lengthy and drawn out process, we have broken this publication into finely executed short chapters, chock full of information that is easily digestible and quick to learn and understand. There is nothing I loathe more than taking the 7 year path to an easily attainable 4 year venture. The diagrams and additions in the back of the book are easy to follow and view for continued access to the valuable information imparted.

Sixteen years ago, I jumped from the wonderful world of garbage and waste hauling, (yes you are reading that correctly) into the fascinating realm of Etiquette. Since then, I have taken great pride and joy in discovering its place in society and most importantly, educating and spreading civility to others wherever I can. I have had the pleasure to work, meet, and collaborate with many skilled and knowledgeable etiquette experts during this fabulous journey I have embarked upon.

In this book you will hear from some of these experts in the field of etiquette, offering their business expertise on this ever rising title of Executive Presence. Here we will provide not only the definition of it, but the tried and true examples of how to achieve it, believe in it, and transform your career and leadership abilities. As a co-author of several other books myself, I am honored to collaborate with these fine professionals, allowing their voices to be heard via a joint effort. I tip my hat to each of them for their kindness, dedication and willingness to partake in this journey with me.

Nancy Hoogenboom, Danielle Richardson, Carolyn M. Powery, and Leona Johnson have joined collective forces with me for this project with years of experience totaling well over fifty years. I am happy and extremely blessed to call these professionals my colleagues, friends, and fellow business etiquette experts throughout the United States. Please feel free to read about each of them in the BIO section of the book and reach out to them for workshops, training and expert etiquette advice. Each are impeccable with their word, their knowledge, and their ability to impart etiquette wisdom to learners of all ages.

~ Karen Thomas

Poised Polished Professional

THE EXPERTS' GUIDE TO EXECUTIVE PRESENCE

CHAPTER I

EXECUTIVE PRESENCE DEFINED

Models Attorney Neal White, Gina White, Actress
Photos courtesy of Teddy

Poised Polished Professional

Executive Presence Defined

Karen Thomas

Executive Presence is a conglomeration of traits that a leader has learned and now possesses. It is developed over time and it is not something one can choose to title themselves with. One cannot simply proclaim, "I have executive presence". It does not depend upon the number of degrees you hold or positions of prestige you have, but rather the professionalism you EXUDE. How you hold yourself, carry out directives, professionally polish, and most importantly, how you flawlessly and effortlessly allow others to achieve their business successes and goals defines your executive presence. Your style and grace have much to do with it, thus proper etiquette comes into play.

Here are some examples of what some professionals believe falls under the definition of executive presence:

"Executive Presence refers to the quality of a leader who is able to get others to get the job done through good communication and with good intention. This presence includes a quality of being ethical and strong while being kind and respectful of those around him/her. This would encompass being truly professional in how one conducts their day to day activities."

Dr. Tommasina Sideris
www.eyesonlitchfield.com

"Executive Presence, I think of someone who has an ability to command a room with grace, integrity, humility, influence and respect. It goes beyond leadership and has a different quality. As that person walks into the room, their presence is felt. All eyes turn on them. The respect earned by one with Executive Presence creates an energy of collaboration and common vision so that big things can get done."

Holly Wade, CEO of Holly Wade Wellness, Master Trainer of The World GROOVE Movement, Contributor for We Are Beautiful Magazine Radio Host for Living from the Inside Out
www.hollywadewellness.com

"Executive Presence, to me, is someone who embodies leadership and who is a driver for results; someone who is an influencer of people."

Tina Kadish, Freedom Strategist, Speaker, Coach
www.lifeisideal.com

"Executive Presence, to me, The strong presence of a confident human being who exudes power, strength, leadership and genuine love that is felt within the core and souls of others that crossed their paths and Karen Thomas is one of those amazing and beautiful souls.
Dhylles Victoria, Entrepreneur Coach, PR/Social Media Marketing Strategist, Queen of Sip & Chat Movement
www.dhylles.com

While we explore the qualities of executive presence, let's keep in mind some of the traits that all of these professionals seemed to agree on and mention: leadership, influence, and support for others. It might be surprising how etiquette plays such a significant role in the attainment of executive presence. We can all imagine such a significant role in the attainment of executive presence. We can all imagine or remember the experience of sitting through a meeting and observing that one person who enters the room and turns heads, not by their physical beauty, but by their mere positive presence, by the air about them exuding kindness, authority, and trust. The one that makes everyone comfortable before them regardless of their title, the one with impeccable manners, and the one that clearly and simply has attained **EXECUTIVE PRESENCE.**

Etiquette is often referred to as the rules or customary code of polite behavior in society or a particular profession or group. It is highly recommended to learn the "ins and outs" of etiquette, especially in the business arena, as it will often take you places where even the highest forms of education will not suffice. Simply stated, your manners and mannerisms are key in becoming a leader. Knowing how to network, converse, dine, compose a document, or even run a meeting all have etiquette rules behind them. While most may appear to be simple pleasantries or stuffy formalities, they exist and continue to be upheld for reasons of civility and a higher level of presence. These are not to make anyone uncomfortable or to distance anyone who is ignorant of etiquette practices, but instead function to make things run smoother and offer a professional atmosphere. In other words making yourself more **POISED**, **POLISHED**, and **PROFESSIONAL** will simply guide you UP the ladder of success, leadership, and executive roles.

Refinement of such qualities is key in becoming recognized as one with executive presence. Therefore, knowing how to dine, enter a room, exude confidence and grace, carry on conversations, run meetings etc… perfectly and flawlessly sends you on your way to leadership roles, increased clientele, and most importantly increased bottom lines.

Striving to exude a professional presence encompasses many things but can be broken down into what we will call the Three Pillars of Executive Presence:

I   Gravitas
II Communication
III Appearance

We will explore each pillar in-depth with simple ways to achieve these core competencies. With continued practice you will become the Poised, Polished, Professional that everyone strives to become.

> *Think about it this way, it is always more pleasant to dine with someone who executes a dinner meeting effortlessly. You know, the one who invites you out for a client dinner, is there when you arrive, inquires of your dietary restrictions ahead of time, ensures that you are comfortable, allows you to feel at ease during the dinner meeting and then offers a follow up for a later date to confirm any business transacted at said dinner. This meeting also leaves you with a good feeling that you accomplished something, enjoyed the company (even though it was business) and left you confident with your business transaction.*

Poised Polished Professional

Chapter II
Pillar I – Gravitas

Poised Polished Professional

Chapter II
Pillar I – Gravitas

Karen Thomas

Let us first define confidence as a feeling of self-assurance arising from one's appreciation of their own abilities or qualities. What is it that you put out there as a confident individual? A confident individual shows how you feel about others (positivity a big player here), shows that you are not afraid to be wrong, asserts a leadership power and increased sense of knowledge, maintains a positive mindset even in the most negative of situations or lack of civility, attracts individuals to you and your stance, shows you are a good listener, does not seek limelight and rather seeks to add to others shine, is not afraid to ask for help, does not put others down, accepts and owns their mistakes, displays exemplary body language, and speaks clearly and slowly. Adopting these traits will allow you to begin the process of exuding professional presence.

When I enter a room as an etiquette expert ready to teach a large group of college students, I exude confidence. So what exactly do I look like?

Good Posture

Smiling

Eye Contact

Welcoming Stance

One of the first things people note about me when they meet me is my posture and confidence upon entering a room. When introduced to people as an etiquette expert, the immediate reaction from others is to adjust their stance or sit up straighter and I often sense a bit of anxiety for fear that I am going to point out their flaws. However, the first thing learned by all etiquette educators is to never point out others flaws or mistakes. With the entire premise behind etiquette being respect for self and others, when speaking in front of a group of people, I state first and foremost, "please be yourself and enjoy my presentation". This usually allows another shuffle of people adjusting their seating and smiling even more as they are allowed to feel comfortable and recognize that I am there to educate and not to humiliate!

However, with that being said, the simple example I set for others by standing up straight, offering welcoming body language, making eye contact, and smiling allows for others to be at ease. By the end of my presentations, I notice a greater sense of confidence exuded by the attendees as they mirror my stance. They become more aware of how my confidence is contagious and offers a positive manner for all to approach.

So go forth with a confident smile, stance, body language and positive attitude. Exude your confident traits each and every day.

Confidence
Nancy Hoogenboom

People want to follow people who are confident, think of someone who you have been attracted to for their confidence. At a meeting a few years ago, a women named Lauren who was confident in her demeanor impressed me. After the meeting, I approached Lauren and shared how I appreciated her leadership skills. As time went by, Lauren became my mentor and it all started with her confidence. So what is this confidence that we are so drawn to?

Merriam-Webster Dictionary defines confidence as "a feeling or consciousness of one's powers or of reliance on one's circumstances". Synonyms for confidence are aplomb, assurance, self-assurance, self-assuredness, self-confidence, self-esteem, self-trust.

> *"What lies behind you and what lies in front of you, pales in comparison to what lies inside of you."*
>
> ~ Ralph Waldo Emerson

While attending a networking luncheon I happened to sit by a woman who did the hiring for her company. As I shared about my company, Daily Etiquette, she immediately shared a story regarding her hiring process for her successful company. The conversation was profound- before she hired anyone, the last interview would be at a nice restaurant enjoying a meal. If the interviewer passed "the test" then they would be hired. This intrigued me so I asked her, "what was she looking for", her answer was profound. "I look for how the person treats each and everyone they come in contact with, no matter who they are. You may present yourself as well groomed and dress impeccably, but how we treat others is most important." As I reflected on her words, I realized that a person who treats others well is one who is comfortable in his or her own self – in other words, a confident person.

> *"Action is a great restorer and builder of confidence. Inaction is not only the result, but the cause, of fear. Perhaps the action you take will be successful; perhaps different action or adjustments will have to follow. But any action is better than no action at all."*
>
> ~ Norman Vincent Peale

Confidence comes from within

Sharpening your inner voice with positive self-talk is important in business. You could be starting a new career or you could be taking a step up in your career, each of these requires confidence to get the most out of your work and social life. Positive self-talk is crucial to being productive through the day. Forming habits of affirmations is a proven method to help with self-improvement. Affirmations are positive statements to reprogram our negative self-talk to more positive thinking. Think of affirmations as exercise for our minds, similar to exercises to improve our physical health. Many times we might be thinking "there is no way I am able to get everything done today". Instead we can start with an affirmation to begin the day on a positive note. You will be surprised how helpful this exercise can be. One affirmation on a full day of work could be, "I will get through this day one task at a time. I know I can accomplish anything I set my mind to."

> *"Confidence comes from discipline and training."*
>
> ~Robert Kiyosaki

A friend shared her experience about confidence with me. When she walks into her college classroom to start teaching a new class, she always feels anxious. As an introvert, she is not one who naturally feels confident in front of people, even though she has been teaching at the college level for over ten years. Knowing this, she takes steps to project confidence even though inside she feels some anxiety about the new situation. Those steps include choosing clothing that is comfortable and professional, smiling as she enters the classroom, and making eye contact with students as they enter the room. She also reminds herself that she is there to teach, something that she knows how to do. Rather than being a case of "faking it until you make it," her actions help to remind her of the reality of her years of experience and of her ability to teach.

> *"Confidence is contagious. So is lack of confidence."*
>
> ~Vince Lombardi

Confidence and courage go hand in hand. Together, these positive strengths will help you persevere through the roller coaster of life. Years ago I read Failing Forward by John C. Maxwell and found that he redefines failure and success as an opportunity to learn and grow. We are stronger because of our failures, as long as we fail forward. Great and mighty things are accomplished in life when you are confident and use obstacles as opportunities and upsets as a way to redirect your energy.

Being prepared is an important part of confidence. When one is prepared one finds oneself ready to handle work and life situations. Preparedness is being on time. Recently, I was in charge of leading a meeting, however I did not plan for adequate time to travel to the location. While I did text to inform another attendee that I would be tardy, the message was never received. When I arrived at the meeting a few minutes late, everyone was kind in regards to my tardiness. I still felt distracted, unprepared, and not at all confident. If I had allowed extra time I would of have been able to enter the room with a satisfactory level of assurance.

Preparedness also means showing up ready. This entails being groomed, wearing correct clothing attire (better to be overdressed than underdressed, you can always take off a tie, but you can't add one), having electronic devices fully charged, and a positive attitude ready to be a team player will have one enter fully confident. You control situations instead of letting them control you when you are prepared for the day.

> *"Somehow I can't believe that there are any heights that can't be scaled by a man who knows the secret of making his dreams come true. This special secret, it seems to me, can be summarized in four C's. They are curiosity, confidence, courage, and constancy, and the greatest of these is confidence. When you believe in a thing, believe in it all the way."*
>
> ~ WALT DISNEY

Increasing Your Self Confidence

Some people are born with a positive attitude, but others can certainly learn how to have confidence. Below are some helpful ways to increase your self-confidence:

- Being aware of your negative self talk and choosing postive self talk to change, will benefit your physical and mental health.

- Be in control of your self-confidence: Self-confidence is knowing things will go well, it's knowing you have the confidence to handle situations even when uncertainty enters.

- Prepare for a confident day, this means, groom yourself, dress nicely (even if you work from home), wear a smile, listen to positive music as you commute to the office.

- Live by your values and principles. For me, "Treat others as I want to be treated" is one of my core values.

- Correct posture.

- Recognize behavior in confident people, learn and apply their behavior to yours.

- Being poised and polished will make you confident!

- Be grateful, name 5 things you are grateful for daily!

- Listen to inspirational podcasts when getting ready for the day or traveling.

- Be organized in your daily routine.

- Use "Magic Words" daily: "Please", "Thank-you", "May I", "I'm sorry" and "Excuse me" are the top five words. Being polite demonstrates confidence.

Small things become the large things in life. This is extremely true regarding confidence. When you choose to be confident in small areas of business, it is easier to be confident in the larger areas. An example of this in my life is when I began teaching etiquette as a hobby to help others become more confident in life skills. The feedback from others was extremely positive.

Many people asked my advice on etiquette, I received questions regarding business, social, and weddings to name some areas. As I was presented with opportunities to speak at a university, practicum, and other exciting engagements about etiquette; my confidence grew to "I am ready to take this hobby and begin an etiquette business," after discussing with my husband we chose to start Daily Etiquette.

> *"Being glamorous is about strength and confidence.*
> *It's black and white—dramatic.*
> *You have to be strong."*
>
> ~ CATHERINE ZETA-JONES

Increasing your self confidence daily in small ways will add up over time to you feeling confident in many situations. Knowing your personal values and goals in life and accepting new challenges will help build your confidence. To be successful in life is to be confident in spite of imperfections. Confidence is a state of mind which helps you move forward in life despite past failures. Remember to fail forward!

Decisiveness
Karen Thomas

Decisiveness is the simple ability to make thoughtful decisions quickly and effectively. A well thought out decision is the key to a successful outcome. However, not every decision you make will be a life changer. For example: what you have for lunch is not as important as the fact that you actually eat lunch. This decision is not a life changer, but can have an adverse effect on decisions later in the day. To take it a bit further – you know your stomach does not tolerate tacos and will upset your stomach later in the day during that important pitch meeting you have…BUT your head is saying – I want tacos for lunch. Be decisive, choose wisely while keeping in mind an idea of the most positive outcome as your day progresses.

Let's be honest, making decisions can be hard. But planning out an important decision is always a good idea when it comes to making a decision that holds more brevity. Make lists, weigh options, and look at the pros and cons. Adopting a clear process for decision making can aid in its ease of implementation. Decisions require focused thinking and even discussing options at length. Accept the fact that there may be risks involved, but don't let information overload take over.

Practice decision making daily. Even the easier ones, such as what to have for lunch or where to host the next meeting, will allow you to become more skilled at the larger ones. The confidence that comes from declaring a decision will boost your enthusiasm and aid in the next decision.

Tips for Decisiveness in Business Situations

- *Gather as much information as possible.*
- *List Pro & Cons*
- *Factor in Past Decisions (if applicable)*
- *Prepare for a desired outcome*
- *Go with your instinct*
- *Rely on your confidence in the ability to make great decisions*
- *Don't talk yourself out of it*

Confidence again, plays a huge role in decisiveness. Put yourself in a leadership role and be confident about your decisions. Being able to back yourself up with facts, lists, and information in your mind makes for a great confidence booster. Speaking factually and slowly will also allow you to get your point across easier and be understood, thus aiding others in being confident in your decisions as well.

Gravitas Integrity
Danielle Richardson

I. Integrity – How to Stand?

When buying a home, there are so many marvelous things to focus on such as an extravagant countertop design and a massive walk-in closet just to name a few. However, before setting your eyes on these luxuries let's direct your focus to the home's foundation. After all, it is what holds up the house. Homeowners need to be able to recognize the different signs of foundation problems because the longer you wait to treat visible signs of damage, the more severe the damage can become. Untreated minor cracks can turn into severe structural issues. Your home's structural integrity depends on the strength of your foundation. It supports everything else – walls, windows, floors, doorways, roof – so when your infrastructure is damaged, it can cause serious problems throughout your home.

What do a home's foundation and integrity have in common? They both need a solid foundation to stand. Equivalent to the standing of a home's walls, windows, floors, doorways, and roof; without integrity, it will be challenging to hold all other gravitas traits such as *confidence, decisiveness, emotional intelligence,* and vision. When I began journeying into the exciting realm of personal and professional development, I spent several years creating a solid foundation. Building a solid foundation consisted of certain habits and skills that I at first was not comfortable with doing. But I knew it was now time to transition my hopeful desires into a fulfilling reality. How do you do so without comprising the values you have set? Is it possible to be productive and successful leader without cutting corners? In business, you cannot talk about etiquette without including ethics or integrity. Our behavior or moral values define us, positively or negatively. Throughout this section, I will highlight examples of incredible integrity-driven leaders who had reputations for building solid foundations and staying true to their values. As for my own experience, now with each new goal I establish or challenge I face, I already have a solid foundation laid that helps my burden to be much lighter. Committing some time to build a foundation of integrity might seem excessive to a few. However, in the long run, it is minimal compared to the reward of being proactive and diligent.

Now that we understand the importance of a solid foundation I will discuss why building a framework based on *integrity* is essential to your overall executive presence. The Webster dictionary definition of the word integrity is the "soundness of moral character." I suggest *integrity* is more than just being honest. The foundation or root word for integrity is an *integer (a whole number)*, which means wholeness, soundness, and completeness. That means you must be true to your authentic self or who you are as a person in the face of pressure. According to the author Dr. Myles Monroe, "when you are one [your authentic self] people eventually trust you, and your word is always good. You say what you said, do what you said, and act what you said". Integrity takes having high moral principles and an accuracy of one's actions. Integrity cannot be compromised, bribed, or based on circumstance. Every day we are faced with decisions that reflect our integrity. You may have desired integrity in yourself, family, and even in the people with whom you work. We see people today who often base their integrity on situational bases.

For instance, in 2009, Volkswagen found themselves in the midst of trying to cover up emissions fraud in their cars, which was deemed one of the largest business scandals of all time. Investigators found that the vehicles falsely showed emissions meeting standards. The test covered 11 million cars manufactured and sold by Volkswagen worldwide. Instead of owning up to the mistake early, many excuses were used to cover up the error. Why did they believe they could get away with allowing engineers to cheat the emissions industry methodically? A lack of integrity can be concluded. Integrity starts from the top down. Senior leaders have a responsibility to model and train others in ethical codes of conduct. Establishing a foundation of integrity is similar to that of a home, and thus any small cracks left unchecked can become significant.

On the other hand, let's take a look at Starbucks Company, which is one of the worlds most recognized brands. There was a period when Starbucks went through a major branding crisis and serious competition surrounded them. In 2008, upon Howard Schultz second return as CEO, he openly admitted to their leadership errors by standing in front of 180,000 Starbucks people and their families confessing that leadership had failed. He shut the doors of more than 7,000 stores for three and a half hours to retrain employees on the company's values and quality expectations. In this case, the number of sales that were lost was not as significant as the importance of instilling proper codes of conduct. After owning to leaderships mistake and creating a practical Transformation Agenda, Starbucks Company was able to efficiently create a powerful turning point without defiling the integrity of the company.

Those who lack standards of integrity may sacrifice whatever principles and values that they hold. We must ask ourselves, do I have any small integrity issues that are left unchecked? How do people perceive me? Do my words match my actions? Integrity plays a key role in a leader's ability to be effective. A leader who exhibits integrity will move smoothly, earn and keep the trust of those around them. We cannot be genuinely authentic without integrity.

II. Unraveling Integrity

Great leaders have certain qualities that are difficult to classify. Have you ever met someone you've felt very comfortable with talking to about almost anything? When this person walks into the room, they seem to have the "it" factor. An extremely sought after trait with personal and professional development is Executive Presence. Executive presence is the most essential element in effective leadership. Simply put, executive presence refers to having the ability to engage, inspire, bring focus, and transform so that people may act. When you have character qualities such as authenticity and honesty, it helps to build trust. The role integrity plays in executive presence is very significant. Based on the integrity of your character people will either be drawn to you or deterred from you. I suggest these three principles that can help strengthen your foundation of integrity without the compromising of your values.

1. Transitioning from the Inside Out

Executive presence takes a lot of effort both outward and inward, though we can find that the outside is easier to work on than the inside. I've interacted with people who, at first, look like they have it all together but through time their true character was revealed. When focusing on the outward self, you can certainly give away a persona of professionalism or success. According to Steve Covey, the author of 7 Habits of Highly Effective People, "if there isn't deep integrity and fundamental character strength, the challenges of life will cause true motives to surface and human relationship failure will replace short-term success." So, let's look at this for a moment. I will share a true story that will paint a clear picture of how comprising your integrity affects you and those around you.

Many are familiar with the notorious Al Capone's story, but not many know about his lawyer who was so skilled at keeping Al Capone out of jail that he was given the name Easy Eddie. Al showed his appreciation for Eddie by giving him huge sums of money and a house that covered an entire block in the city of Chicago. Eddie lived such a luxurious life that he only gave little thought to the evils that surrounded him. Eddie was a lawyer but also a father who ensured his son had everything in life to get him ahead. Despite his lack of integrity due to his involvement in organized crime, he had a goal to teach his son right from wrong and to be a better man than he was. Due to his lifestyle, there was something that Eddie could not teach his son and that was integrity. Eventually, Eddie decided to right his wrongs. He went to the law enforcement admitting to the crimes of Al Capone in hopes to clean up his name and offer some aspect of integrity to his son. This led to Eddie testifying against Al Capone and within a year his life ended. In his eyes, he had given the greatest gift he could to his son – integrity.

As a leader your integrity, or lack thereof, is the most important example you can set to those around you. When confronted with the question "What good is it for a man to gain the whole world and lose his own soul," how would you answer this? Eddie entered into a profession in which he was expected to uphold the law but chose to enrich himself in unethical schemes. Eddie had the persona, the house, the family, and the job. From the outside looking in he appeared to be a very wealthy and successful man. But on the inside, I can only imagine the strong conviction and paranoia that he suffered each day.
In order to have executive presence we must start by defining our core values. Knowing your values will tell you when you are uncomfortable in a situation. It tells you when not to compromise. When you don't meet your values, it will be bothering you. Make integrity a core value. Core values support your mission either for yourself or company.

2. Perception

We all may know someone that possess confidence or charisma, but we may have a hard time trusting them due to their perception of dishonesty or selfish motives. Integrity has an impact on the perceived executive presence, and lack thereof can be hard to overcome and may hurt one's executive presence. People who give the perception of having integrity with only their words may give a false impression if their actions do not match their words. That delivers a perception that they cannot be trusted. Your perception has a profound effect on how people see you. People's perceptions are shaped by what they observe or have directly experienced. It is our thoughts that determine our behaviors and actions, which lead to the perception others have of us. An employee perception of a senior leader's integrity can be based on their commitments being in line with their actions, fair decision-making, and being upfront about any changes or mistakes. If there is a lack of integrity within an organization the perception will be dissonant. The right perception is vital because others will make decisions based on the perception an organization transmits.

3. Enactment

Enactment is the process of acting something out. Integrity has less to do with words and more to do with actions. We must maintain integrity by being honest and ethical, always admitting the truth, and not being afraid to say, "I don't know." If you create a habit of doing what you say, then your light will continue to shine and if you make it a habit of breaking promises your light goes out. Keeping in mind the story of "Easy Eddie," pay close attention to this example of how integrity affects those around you.

During World War II there was an honorable hero name Lieutenant Butch O'Hare who was a fighter pilot. While on an airborne mission he realized just after takeoff that his fuel tank had not been topped off with fuel. As a result, he would not be able to complete his mission and get back to the ship. Therefore, he dropped out of formation and followed the orders of his commander who told him to return to the ship. On his way back, he was alarmed as he witnessed Japanese planes speeding toward an American fleet he just left. Due to the mission, the American fleet was defenseless and Lt. O'Hare had no time warn the fleet of the approaching danger. Without taking into account his safety he decided to divert them from the fleet by diving into the formation of the Japanese planes blazing his guns. Although he and his plane were wounded, he did not give in. Surprised by the act, the Japanese planes took off in another direction. Upon his return to the ground, the film from the gun-camera that was mounted on the plane told his entire tale and showed the extent of Butch's heroism. He destroyed 5 enemy aircrafts. Butch became the Navy's first Ace of World War II and the first Naval Aviator to win the Congressional Medal of Honor. In his memory, the O'Hare Airport in Chicago was named after his bravery. What's even more surprising? Butch O'Hare was "Easy Eddie's" son.

Although Lt. Butch O'Hare heroism is highlighted, he was known as a man of integrity, unlike his father. He was able to redeem his family name through his bravery. In the O'Hare Airport in Chicago, there is a memorial in recognition of his bravery. Integrity takes courage. Maybe not to the extent of Lt. O'Hare, but your willingness to move forward despite the probable cost will highlight your integrity. You can enact integrity by keeping your commitments, making fair decisions, and communicating honestly.

Every day we are faced with small or large choices in doing or acting out what is right for a particular situation. As leaders, we have an undying strive for excellence at whatever we do. That is why with each new task there must be a solid foundation laid. People will either be attracted or deterred from you based on the integrity of your character along with your skills. When people are drawn to you your business grows, skills grow, and knowledge grow. You become the type of person people want to follow. Integrity creates cohesion among others and is necessary for a healthy business. Etiquette is more than just knowing how to shake hands or reading a company's policy and procedures. Protocol, as it relates to integrity, will guide you to unfamiliar conditions and help you know what to expect from others. We must remember that a reputation of integrity is slowly gained but quickly lost.

Poised Polished Professional

Vision

Danielle Richardson

I. What is Vision?

Do you have a thought-out vision that will impact your life, organization, and those around you? I remember a specific moment in my life when I didn't have a vision or a plan. I was so busy working on a project and moving so fast that the hours, days, weeks, and months had left before my eyes. I would finally look up to ask myself, "how did I get here?" After all, it wasn't like I spent all my time watching television for hours. Consider a time while making your morning commute to work, you immediately snap out of a daze, look around, and realize you've driven all the way to your destination without noticing it. It's somewhat frightening when you think about, but it happens. That is the same feeling you acquire when there is no real productivity done throughout the day. I was just "busy" doing a lot more without getting a lot more done. I knew then that there was a void. I lacked vision and a clear plan, which caused me to settle for what I thought was useful rather than the great possibilities awaiting me. In this chapter, we will define vision as it relates to an executive presence, then identify strategies to target and communicate your vision to others, and finally, you will discover how to articulate your vision to carry it out from a vision to reality.

> *"The difference between a vision and a dream is stewardship."*
>
> ~Danielle Richardson

Developing a vision will provide you with an authentic executive presence. If you desire to be respected and followed, then having proper etiquette as it relates to this gravitas trait is necessary. Etiquette is merely a set of guidelines that govern good behavior but can also enhance your status at work, as you will be perceived as more professional, more capable, and more intelligent. Therefore, etiquette will play an impactful role in developing a vision. Vision is an inspiring idea of what your world or organization should be like. It creates a desire to grow and improve. When a vision is manifested with action, your vision then comes to life. A vision can reflect the dream of a founder or leader of the business. For instance, Amazon's vision is "to be earth's most customer-centric company; to build a place where people can come to find and discover anything they might want to buy online." A vision must be clear and concise so that the organization can have a clear understanding and purchase into its passion. The inspiring author, Helen Keller, states, *"the only thing worse than being blind is having sight but no vision."* Sight is a function of what the eyes can naturally see. If we rely only on our sight, then the way things are is all we will see. For instance, if you are one of many applicants on a brink for a promotion, your sight may allow you to focus on the competition rather than the unlimited possibilities that may be in store for you. Vision, on the other hand, looks at future possibilities of how things should or could be like. You may believe in yourself for this promotion so much that you have already started training your replacement. That's vision!

> *"Those with sight alone will end wherever the road takes them. Those with vision will end up somewhere purposefully."*
>
> ~ DANIELLE RICHARDSON

Soaring remarkably high in the sky, the Eagle is known to have an extremely keen vision with the ability to see in detail five times further than a person with perfect vision. Much like the characteristics of a "visionary", an eagle can see something many others don't see. It can spot its prey from afar thus keeping its enemies away from their nests. They are commonly known to sit in high places, watching attentively. According to the author, Dr. Myles Munroe, pigeons scavenge on the ground and grumble and complain all day long while eagles fly and make less noise. We as visionaries are influenced to lead and mount up with wings like eagles to soar with vision and courage.

Vision is the key to excellent leadership. As a visionary, we can learn a lot about vision from the eagle. Many successful leaders, current and historical, had a clear and concise vision in common which helps led to their success. Why does developing a vision matter? Life is a journey and within the journey is a process. Whether we notice if we are driving or not, every journey has a destination. Those with sight will end wherever the road takes them. Those with vision will end up somewhere on purpose. Creating a vision will bring your world or organization into a more structured focus. When great is an option, why settle for good?

II. Targeting Your Vision with a Purpose

A compelling vision is critical for establishing goals whether personal development or the development of an organization. Understanding vision is one thing, but now we must make your vision a little more tangible. We will look into strategies that will enable you, with the essentials needed, to move from wishful thinking to strategic planning and implementation that produces results.

1. Shift your paradigm

A *"paradigm"* is the way you see the world. In other words, it is how we view what we think is normal. A *"paradigm shift"* enables you to view the world in a different way or different point of view. In many circumstances, a paradigm shift can shift your focus to see a new perspective that enables you to analyze a situation much better. To shift paradigms, you must first break through mental barriers. Unwillingness to assess the full understanding of a situation can hinder you from seeing the world in a different light. In the book, "7 Habits of Highly Effective People", Stephen Covey impeccably explains that we tend to see the world objectively, but we actually see the world not as it is, but as we are – or as we are conditioned to see it. Therefore, what we interpret as "right" is created through our own personal experiences without properly questioning its accuracy. We must be able to keep up with the shifts in paradigms to successful increase the effectiveness of our executive presence. In business, new paradigms can lead to innovative leadership. If you are not aware of the shift in your industry, then you should be.

2. Paint a Picture

How do you want to live? How do you want your story to end? Using the example from earlier, when I lost track of purpose while occupying my time with busy work, I later realized that I had to add structure to the way I handled goal setting. Having a destination with no plan to get there can be chaos. So I began painting a detailed picture in my mind of what I expected for my life.

Painting a picture of your vision means to transfer it from your thoughts to a simple detailed description. It is a plan used to help express your vision of an ideal future. When transferring your vision from your thoughts to a tangible source, you will have the opportunity to see in detail what you want out of your life or organization. A picture is worth a thousand words, so when you paint a picture of something, it has the power to change you greater than just merely "thinking" about it. Your life will become what you focus on so we must train our brains to execute the vision. Take a moment and close your eyes and imagine what you want for your life. Ask yourself, what is my desired reality? Then envision yourself from the end result to where you are now. What career objectives do you see? To exhibit your executive presence within an organization, people are motivated when they can see a clear vision. When they see it, the more likely they are to believe it is possible. The more details you give, the more realistic the future will be to them. You may use visuals, diagrams, written statements, and pictures to help articulate your vision.

3. Speak like a Visionary

Articulating your vision is vital when leading people. It takes more than just having a dream or a great idea. Your leadership potential will be determined by how well you express to your audience the passion for your cause. As a leader, you will need to articulate an ambitious view of the future and be able to justify the transformation. How do your recommendations impact those in the room? Who will benefit? According to Sylvia Hewlett, the author of Executive Presence, "excellent leaders possess vision – the ability to see possibilities and communicate them to others". You may not be the most articulate or persuasive person, but if your vision is clear and people believe in it, you can become a leader that others want to follow. Abraham Lincoln, Martin Luther King Jr., and Gandhi are three leaders that have led their worlds with a vision. People simply believed in their vision that they courageously shared with others.

In order to articulate a vision that will influence followers you must keep your vision inspirational, ambitious, realistic, creative, descriptive, clear, and consistent. Let's take a look at one of the most visionary leaders that foreseen the future of technology, Steve Jobs of Apple. I recently ran across a Forbes article that highlighted an interview with Steve Jobs. The question was asked, "What is your vision for the personal computer? According to the interviewer, "Steve Jobs was a magical storyteller and for the next hour, he talked about how personal computers were going to change the world. He painted a picture of how it would change everything about the way we worked, educated our children and entertained ourselves. You couldn't help but buy in." Vision, was the one thing that separated Steve Jobs from the others. He took a picture he had in his mind and effectively communicated it which motivated employees to make revolutionary product and services. When introducing a new product he spoke with excitement and passion so much that customers was mesmerized by his message. Steve Jobs didn't just sell products; he sold dreams and accomplished this by speaking like a visionary.

III. From Vision to Reality

As visionary leaders, we are pioneers. We guide our followers to new and unexplored territories. Some leaders do not gain the respect or followers they desire because they keep changing the vision. Although your vision may grow and you adjust it over time, you must be clear about what is deeply important to you and pursue it passionately. We have learned that being a visionary leader comes from developing specific skills and ways of looking at the world. It is something every one of us can learn to do better. The following highlights proved practices that are found successful in making a vision transform into reality.

Set Goals. To make your vision reality, you need to have a clear goal to start if you want to achieve it. Write it down and set a date for when your vision will be a reality. If focusing on the overall picture is too overwhelming, direct your focus to your next step.

Be Bold. Face and embrace your fear. Take your power back and make calculated risks. Courage can transform ordinary leaders into impactful visionaries.

Be Intentional. Incorporate your vision into your everyday life. Whatever you do throughout the day, act as if the vision is already happening. Talk as if you have already made plans to travel where you want, promoted to the position you greatly desire, started the business you have been passionate about starting.

Make Mistakes. When you fail, look for the lesson and learn from the mistakes and try again. We all failed at some point in our lives or the lives of our organizations. Fail your way to success and expect to succeed.

Poised Polished Professional

Chapter III
Pillar II--
Communication Conversation, Cell & Phone Etiquette

Models Attorney Neal White, Gina White, Actress
Photos courtesy of Teddy

Poised Polished Professional

Chapter III
Pillar II-- Communication
Conversation, Cell & Phone Etiquette

Communication
Carolyn M. Powery

Effective communication is a very important part in business. Communication is used to assert one's self authentically, articulate directives as a leader, connect globally, exchange information, make a good first impression and professional presence. The two types of communication methods leaders use daily in the business world are verbal and nonverbal communication.

We live in a technological world where information is only a click away. Proper communication etiquette in the workplace allows others to show politeness, courtesy, respect, and manners toward each other. Be intentional in how you want to come across as a communicator in the business world.

Behaviors that do not represent proper communication etiquette in the business world are:
- Rude interruption of others during conversation
- Disrespectful loud talk outside someone's office
- Gossiping
- Cell phone distractions
- Profanity

Communication Faux Pas

At a prestigious oil company, John, a lower-level manager in the field, has impeccable communication and leadership skills. During a training session he was attending, the Vice President noticed his ability to express himself professionally. He was impressed and promoted him to lead trainer at Corporate. The difference in field work and Corporate was night and day. John quickly found out profanity in the corporate office was unacceptable and could result in immediate dismissal. Corporate suggested he take a business etiquette workshop in professionalism and communication. John ceased using profanity. He used alternative words. He recognized the negativity vulgar language creates in the workplace. Self-examination of his new role allowed him to re-image others' perception of him as a leader.

How to Communicate Effectively

Effective communication in business is essential in building your career and securing your next client. Being a good listener and making others feel that you care about their message is another aspect of effective communication. Face-to-face communication has transitioned into use of cell phones, Skype, texting, emailing, webinars, teleconferencing, and social media. However, meeting in person is still the most important form of communication. Nothing compares to the human connection and the ability to use all your senses to evaluate verbal and nonverbal cues.

As a professional, it is imperative to be conscientious of the messages you relay. For example, you have expressed verbally your excitement about a new project assigned to you, but your body language does not reflect enthusiasm. Your verbal and nonverbal cues should match. Approximately 93% of how you are judged is based on nonverbal cues.

The Three V's of Communication: Visual, Vocal, and Verbal

According to Psychologist Albert Mehrabian, people perceive what they hear and see rather than what you say. This is not to say that your words don't matter, but visual and vocal are what people connect with first. The visual accounts for 55% of the body language and appearance, vocal is 38%, and 7% is your verbal message. Visual is what your audience sees: Your eye contact, body language, facial expression, visual presentation, appearance, and attire. Vocal is your voice quality, tone of voice, and speed of voice. Verbal is the message you communicate.

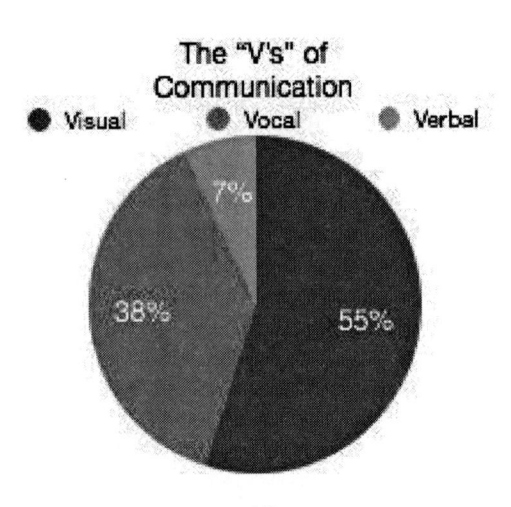

The "V's" of Communication

- Visual
- Vocal
- Verbal

- Visual: 55%
- Vocal: 38%
- Verbal: 7%

Mastering the art of communication is crucial in showing executive presence as a leader. Whether you are engaged in a one-on-one conversation, conducting a meeting, doing an interview, or speaking to an audience, effective communication requires the same effort. A charismatic leader connects and influences people.

Tips to Consider when Developing your Communication Skills

Have Confidence

Your ability to think outside the box with confidence is a huge move toward achieving executive presence. You have to believe in yourself in order to persuade others into action. Confidence with preparedness will equal success.

Practice, Practice, and Practice

I teach my clients to visualize in detail what they are wearing, their rate of breathing, body language, the audience, the room setup, and the way they are speaking. This exercise helps you to feel more confident and comfortable. I teach my female clients to practice walking the stage in heels. This promotes a commanding presence and confident body language. Additional tips are to practice in the mirror and record your voice to evaluate your tone and speed.

The Art of Listening

As a leader, it is important to have excellent listening skills. You don't want to be viewed as a leader who makes poor decisions because you did not listen well enough to gather all the facts. Perfecting this skill will help you in your career advancement. A leader who is an active listener can potentially boost morale because it makes others feel valued.

The Art of Articulation and Communication

Learn to pace the speed of your speech and speak clearly. Avoid talking too fast or slow. This will ensure the listener does not misinterpret your message. When speaking, learn to pause. This will give you an opportunity to gather your thoughts and for your receiver to comprehend your message. Communicate selflessly. Think about the person who is receiving your message.

Avoid Filler Words

Filler words are words that distract from your intended message. Common filler words are um, ah, so, like, I was like oh my God, and you know what I mean. Excessive use of filler words adversely affects your leadership credibility. It sounds as if you are uneducated, unprofessional, and lack confidence.

Tips to eliminate filler words:
- Use the pause method to help eliminate these words.
- Have others to point out when you use filler words
- Become more conscious of the filler words you use and write them down
- Record yourself during presentations or speaking engagements

I routinely record my speaking engagements. After listening to one of my presentations, I discovered my excessive use of the filler word was "so." It was a complete surprise, but it made me conscientious of my overuse of it.

Poise

Leadership is a challenging role. Whether it is a disgruntled customer or employee, or meeting deadlines, your reaction will reveal whether or not you have executive presence. Your ability to stay calm and maintain control of the situation will determine the level of poise.

Demeanor

Your behavior and attitude toward others can adversely affect your message and how you are perceived. Do you lack a warm, approachable personality? Do you smile and make others feel welcoming?

Influence

Do your leadership skills influence others to strive for success, work hard, and go that extra mile on that million dollar contract? People feel good about themselves when they are appreciated.

Clarification

Clarification is a two-way street. Either your message was not clear or the other person's message was not. Don't second guess what you think the message was - ask questions. If you find that the receiver of your message is constantly asking questions, it could be that your messages are not clear. Value the opinion of others.

Being a good leader is not all about you and your opinion. Take into consideration the opinion of others. They may just have a better idea or approach than yours.

Common Executive Presence Questions

Can an introvert develop executive presence? Are you one of the 40% who would like to change their introverted tendencies, but need help? Start with reframing how you see yourself. Imagine yourself as an extrovert who connects with others and attracts others to you. Social media can be a great way to boost your confidence and build relationships. Be bold and step up to the plate. Just put yourself out there. Believe it or not, I am an introvert and I have made tremendous progress in overcoming my shyness. I have made guest appearances on local TV and as a speaker and presenter.

Ways to Communicate Executive Presence as a Woman

- Present yourself as an articulate communicator
- Voice your opinion without hesitation
- Present yourself as a poised woman who handles being under pressure
- Maintain commanding presence in your stance and walk
- Dress polished and professional
- Show confidence and credibility

A 2013 Business Insider article describes executive presence as the 7 C's: Composure, connection, charisma, confidence, credibility, clarity, and conciseness.

Tips for Improving Your Communication Skills

I had a particular client who is a young professional who was working on advancing her career in the engineering field. She was soft-spoken and lacked confidence. During one of our sessions, I helped her improve how she came across. I created a mock interview and recorded it. This exercise gave her the opportunity to hear her responses, tone of voice, and see her body language. She could see where she needed improvement. She recently landed a job in another state after promoting herself on LinkedIn.

Conversation Etiquette - Message and Content

The year 2017 has brought about huge discussions of workplace harassment, sexual harassment, bullying, and racism. Proper conversation etiquette in the workplace should show professionalism, respect for others and self.

What topics are safe subjects of discussion in the workplace?
- Technology
- Local news, weather, and sports
- Holiday plans
- Business-related books and stories
- Travel recommendations
- Latest trends
- Work projects

What topics are considered unprofessional in the workplace?
- Religion
- Politics
- Medical issues
- Distasteful jokes
- Salary compensation
- Anything sexual in nature and terms of endearment words
- Personal subject matters
- Race
- Bullying

The Art of Small Talk

According to Merriam-Webster, small talk is a light or casual conversation.

Tips on Small Talk:
- Be approachable, don't isolate yourself
- Come off as warm and friendly
- Share appropriate stories
- Ask questions that will promote meaningful conversation

You have less than seven seconds to make a first impression. Small talk is something many entrepreneurs shy away from because they feel uncomfortable talking to complete strangers. Mastery of small talk is one of those people skills that can change the trajectory of your career for the better. Whether you are networking, playing golf, or attending a reception, small talk is a great way to break the ice and make meaningful connections. Small talk is used to strategically control how others perceive you. The stories you choose to share will paint a positive or negative picture. What character traits do you want to be associated with you?

Research by the Carnegie Institute of Technology shows that 85% of social connections, promotions, and financial success is in your ability to communicate. Only 15% is in your educational and intellectual ability. A worker who is brilliant but lacks social skills will find retaining employment problematic. Your goal should be to reach a level where you are comfortable and confident communicating at all management levels.

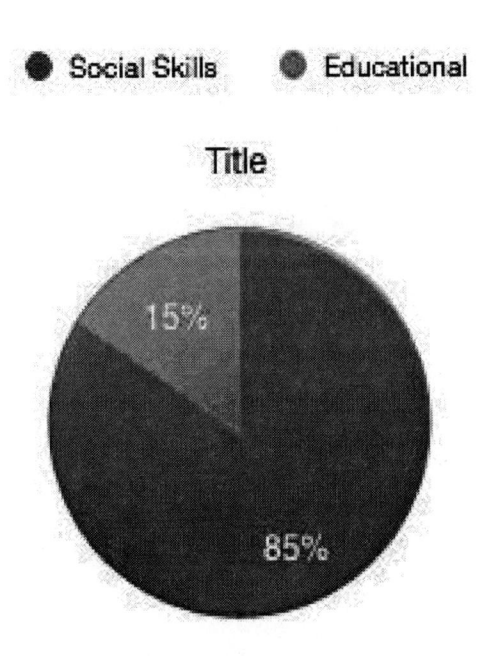

● Social Skills   ● Educational

Title

- 15%
- 85%

What information is appropriate to share during small talk?
- Non work-related topics
- A family vacation trip
- A home project
- A hobby
- Industry-related topics
- Questions related to the other person's company

How important are listening skills when communicating?

Listening skills are crucial in the workplace whether you are conversing with a client over the phone or during a meeting. According to Mark

Wayshak, utilize the 80/20 rule when communicating. Spend 80% of your time listening and 20% of your time communicating your message. You want the other person to feel you actually care about what they are saying. Use "active listening," that is to repeat what the other person said during the conversation.

Six Ways to Maximize Your Listening Skills
- *Make eye contact when you or other person speaks*
- *Give a warm, authentic smile*
- *Show positive body language*
- *Nod and interject or mirror the conversation*
- *Don't monopolize the conversation*
- *Don't interrupt the conversation*

Use of Foreign Language around English Speakers

In the teacher's lounge at school, three Spanish-speaking staff members were having lunch. An African American administrator comes in to have lunch and hears the conversation of them speaking in English. Once the administrator enters the lounge area, they begin to speak in Spanish. The administrator felt uncomfortable and told them to stop speaking in Spanish and that it was rude. They were offended to the point that one of the teachers came in the next day to resign. She felt humiliated and discriminated against. The principal held a meeting with the teacher and the administrator to discuss the issue and it was resolved.

Diversity is very common in the workplace and the goal is for employees to coexist without offending others. In order to avoid conflict, the proper thing to do is to speak the common language. This will prevent others from thinking you may be talking about them and you won't isolate others.

Cell Phone Etiquette

According to a nationwide survey by Kessler International, "untimely and inappropriate use of cell phones" by employees in the workplace is a top pet peeve by upper and middle managers. The fastest way to make a negative impression is to give your cell phone more attention during a face-to-face interaction. Does your professional image show through your cell phone greeting?

Cell phones are a major form of communication to conduct business.

A cell phone greeting is sometimes the first contact a potential client may encounter when dialing your business line. Below are cell phone etiquette strategies.

A professional greeting will create a professional image for your brand

- *Answer your cell phone with a smile*
- *Be respectful of others around you when taking calls, excuse yourself*
- *Be conscious of your voice when answering the phone*
- *Set your cell phone on silent or turn off when discussing business*
- *Return phone calls within 24 hours*

Cell Phone Blunders

- *Taking phone calls during meetings*
- *Being inattentive by focusing on your smart watch or phone*
- *Inappropriate ringtones on a business phone*
- *Answering phone during meetings and instead of utilizing voicemail*
- *Taking selfies during work hours*

A young professional was at work and decided to take a selfie with her phone. Her decision to post the picture turned out to be a violation of policy. Posting the picture also revealed confidential information in the background. Her unprofessional action resulted in immediate termination. Familiarize yourself with company policy regarding use of cell phones.

Telephone Etiquette

In the 21st century telephones in the workplace still play a major part in company operations. Most people today prefer to communicate via text or email. However, if your goal is to secure a leadership position, knowing how to properly and professionally operate a business telephone is imperative to your professional growth. When you answer the phone, you are representing your company or business. Here are some do's and don'ts of telephone etiquette in the workplace.

- *Smile when you answer, use a professional greeting, full name, and company name*
- *Speak clearly and enunciate your words when leaving a message*
- *When calling someone else identify yourself by your first and last*

name, and leave a brief message explaining purpose of your call
- *Always get permission before placing someone on speaker phone*
- *Create a professional voicemail*
- *Respond to phone calls within 24 hours*
- *Avoid answering the phone when eating*
- *Avoid being short with customer or potential client*

Conversation

Karen Thomas

Conversation and the guidelines therein, of forming, speaking and sounding competent while conversing have a wide range. Too often we speak to reply and forego the listening part. A wise person once told me "We were given 2 ears and 1 mouth for a reason"- that being, to listen more and speak less.

Many people utilize the "Speak to Reply" reflex too often without truly hearing the gist, or main point of a thought or conversation in business (personally as well, but that is another topic altogether!). Now I am the first (and my husband will second this!) to admit that I have selective hearing. I have this amazing super power of hearing words come out of my husband or children's mouths, yet not really hearing what they are saying. To me, this super power of hearing the noise, yet not having the faintest idea of what words were said, is just that – a **SUPER POWER**. However, in business that can be a fatal mistake made by most.

One of the first things I teach my etiquette students and clients are tips for sounding professional and carrying on the art of small talk. It is often met with eye rolls with the younger crowd as many have clearly stated – "I know how to talk – is this necessary?" To which my reply is indeed, you also know how to eat, however, do you know how to eat properly for business functions and the proper etiquette therein – Let class begin!" Here, I have provided several tips for Successful Business Conversations:

• **Compliment First** – *This is a great way to open or start a conversation, they provide good feelings toward the person you are engaging with and keep things on a positive note. It is important to note that being specific is key rather than an open ended compliment.*

• **Make Small Talk** – *Staying abreast of current events such as browsing the front pages of your internet provider (Google, Yahoo or whatever homepage you use) is a great way to do so. Using topics such as the meeting or event you are at, as well as the weather will always suffice in a pinch as well. However, please be mindful of taboo subjects such as religion, money, sex, and politics and avoid them at all costs.*

- **Ask Questions** – Most people are happy to talk about themselves, so ask thoughtful questions of them and listen carefully to their answers. The answers given here can be used later on and are key to exuding executive presence flawlessly. Many leaders are able to maintain a plethora of key topics as they relate to others which allows them to be well liked and genuine. It is always a pleasure to speak with someone who remembers thoughtful knowledge.

- **LISTEN** – And do so with open ears and take mental notes. Allow the other person to talk about themselves and engage in what they are saying while showing genuine interest in them.

- **Keep Negativity at Bay** – Keeping the conversation light and positive is key to being a great leader. A good joke or small anecdote is a great way to engage.

- **Be Confident** – Keep body language open to giving and receiving the other person's words and accept others who may want to join in on the conversation.

- **Positive Closing** – If perhaps the conversation seems to be drifting off, boring, or just down right over, just accept the end and close with a positive phrase. "It was great to finally meet in person, I hope we see each other at the event next week." And one final note: if you say you are going to follow up with someone – DO IT. There is nothing worse than someone saying, "Let's grab a coffee soon," with no intentions of ever doing so. This makes for a bad impression afterward and breaks a promise, which is simply not good business.

Cell & Phone Etiquette

In a tech savvy world, you will be hard pressed to find anyone that does not have a smart/cell phone on their person, in their hand, or readily available at a milliseconds notice. Here are some tips for smart cell and office phone adherence:

- *In the office, always answer by the 2nd ring (if possible).*
- *Answer with your full name (Mr. John Doe) and title or department if necessary.*

This allows the caller to know they have reached the correct person without inquiry.
- *Leave thorough information on the voice mail system as to how you may be reached by several options (of your choosing) such as fax, cell or text. It is common to leave a name of a subordinate or colleagues contact information as well if you engage in an extended leave, vacation, etc.*

These small, but rather common sense items complete a full circle of professionalism with such a common subject as phone manners.

Being mindful of our cell habits is a more precise operation and must be monitored more carefully so as not to offend. Never interrupt a face-to-face meeting to take a cellphone call or reply to a text. This indicates that the person calling or texting is much more important than what you were speaking about and may offer high offense. Keep mobile devices off of the meeting and dining tables so that they cannot serve as any sort of distraction or disruption. A pocket, purse or briefcase are a much more suitable place. Placing the device on silent is preferred as well in keeping distractions to a minimum. Nothing screams disinterest more than a person reading their cell phone under a table, and thinking that no one is noticing!

Keep cell usage out of the restroom areas as well. If it is important to take a call immediately, excuse yourself to a private room, a hallway, or outside if a space is available. If you forget to turn off your cell or silence the ringtone, always apologize for the faux pas and do so immediately. Additionally, a professional ringtone is a must rather than a super, fabulous song you just adore which may raise the ire and eyebrows of other executives! Remembering these simple rules will aid in accomplishing the utmost of professionalism.

Netiquette & Paper Correspondence Netiquette

Carolyn M. Powery

What is netiquette? Netiquette are governing rules of behavior over the internet. Twenty-first century netiquette has become an integral part of our personal and professional lives. We are bombarded with new technology. As soon as we learn a new gadget, a new one develops. We are constantly learning and trying to master new forms of communication in the netiquette world. The use of computers has made life so much simpler and faster. Most businesses are operating with computers, laptops, smart phones, and smart watches. Netiquette has had its challenges in the workplaces, resulting in employees losing their jobs because of poor behavior. Many people believe they are protected under the First Amendment to say and post whatever they want on social media.

How you show up online matters. Seventy-eight percent of professionals search online for information on new colleagues or prospective hires. There are pros and cons to posting on social media and you have to decide which perception you want others to have of you.

Cons of Social Media
- Destroys your professional image
- Damages your credibility
- Hurts relationships with clients, donors, or investors
- Job termination
- Hurts your opportunity for promotion

Pros of Social Media Etiquette
- Builds relationships
- Builds credibility
- Increases visibility
- Boosts your changes with donors and investors
- Increases chances for new clients or collaborations
- Increases bottom line

■ Social Media Platforms

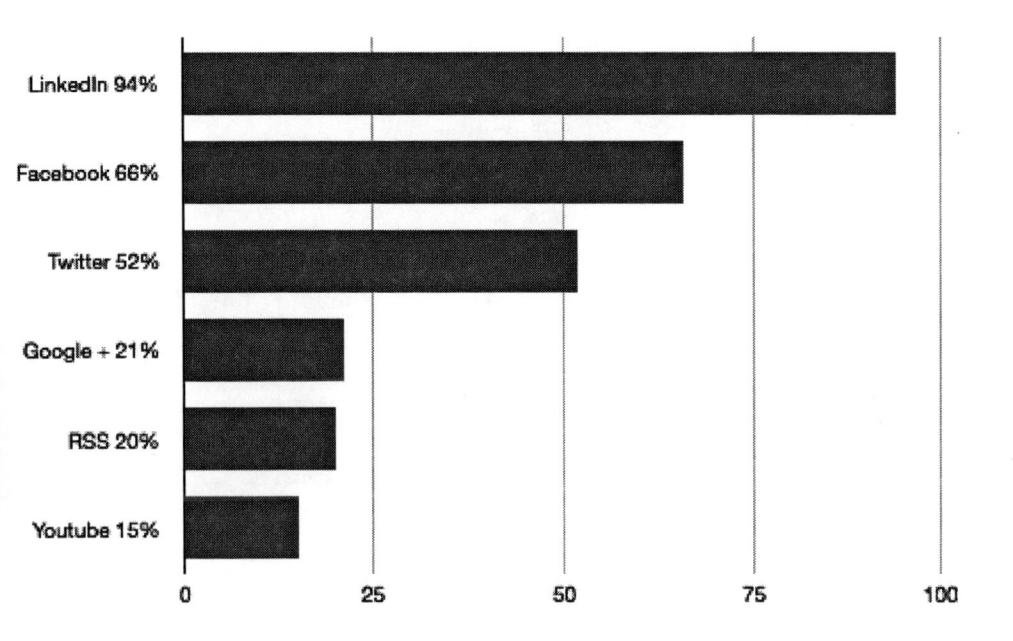

- LinkedIn 94%
- Facebook 66%
- Twitter 52%
- Google + 21%
- RSS 20%
- Youtube 15%

The ABCDE's of Professional Netiquette
- Appearance
- Behavior
- Communication
- Digital Foot Print
- Email Etiquette

Appearance

There is so much noise on social media. Everyone is either trying to get your attention or you are trying to attract your ideal client. Having an online professional presence is an opportunity to position your image as the expert. A picture is worth a thousand words. Whether you are representing your personal brand or your company's brand, your appearance should be taken seriously. The new background check is social media. You are being researched by clients, potential business partners, investors, and human resources. A fast way to kill your professional career is a poor decision to display an unprofessional profile in your social media biography.

Your bio should include your professional name, not an alias. I see so many professionals on LinkedIn with suspicious profiles. They hide behind pictures that have nothing to do with their brand, use avatars for a profile picture, or post inappropriate content and pictures.

A positive first impression is critical to attracting the right clients. A professional headshot is the first contact that a potential business associate sees before meeting you in person. Remember, you are the face of the company. Your photo should consist of a crisp white background. Avoid a busy background. It could give the wrong message. Using an avatar shows poor taste in your professionalism. If you choose to represent your business or company with a video, make sure that the video has excellent lighting and audio. Your social media photo should scream professionalism and prompt others to want to know more about you, your products, and services.

Behavior

Your behavior plays a major factor in how people view you as an expert and professional in your industry. Your attitude is 90% of what people remember about you. Even if you have saved your company thousands of dollars and received recognition for your accomplishments, people will remember your bad decisions before they remember your good ones. In a twinkling of an eye, your career could be turned upside down because of your unprofessional behavior.

What social media faux pas are hurting your personal brand and professional image?

- Posting pictures of you drinking alcohol or doing illegal drugs
- Posting pictures or videos of you dancing wildly
- Insulting others on social media
- Complaining about your boss, customers, or job online
- Making disparaging or false statements about your employer or clients
- Discussing confidential information
- Arguing with internet trolls

The chart below is a breakdown of behaviors to eliminate from your social media profile. According to the 2014 survey conducted by Social Recruiting Survey, 55% of recruiters have reconsidered a candidate based on their social profile, with 61% of those reconsiderations being negative.

POSITIVE NEUTRAL NEGATIVE

	POSITIVE	NEUTRAL	NEGATIVE
Profanity	5%	22%	63%
Spelling/grammar	3%	24%	66%
Illegal drug references	2%	7%	83%
Sexual posts	1%	17%	70%
Volunteering/donations to charity	65%	25%	2%
Political affiliation	2%	69%	17%
Alcohol	2%	43%	44%
Guns	2%	32%	51%

Communication

Before you post online, you should consider how your negative commentary will be viewed by others. Should you take the high road or just post whatever you want? Be selective in your words and messages. Don't compromise your professional image, personal brand, or integrity on social media because you want to practice freedom of speech. Do not be easily provoked into replying or responding to every provocative statement. Sometimes it is best to simply remain silent. In a lot of cases, someone has probably already voiced your opinions anyway. Remember you have a reputation to uphold. As an entrepreneur or professional, everything you do and say online shapes your personal and professional brand. It can hinder or propel your career. You be the judge of how you want to write your story.

Avoid Using Social Media as an Emotional Dumping Ground

Control your emotions and do not be quick to give someone a piece of your mind. Whether you are on social media personally or professionally, refrain from using profanity. What you do during your personal time can affect your professional career. You represent the company you work for on the clock and off the clock.

Avoid being impolite and offensive to others. People are always watching, therefore putting your best foot forward will put you in the safe zone. Avoid sharing your opinions on hot topics. I have seen some heated discussions on social media regarding politics, race, and religion. People are very passionate about these subjects. However, these subjects tend to bring out the worst in people. The safest thing you can do to maintain integrity is to refrain from talking about these subjects. You don't want to risk losing your job or getting promoted.

Social Media Faux Pas

According to entrepreneur.com, a college graduate with a degree in Information Management found out the hard way about posting negative comments on social media about a future employer. After being offered a position from California tech company, Cisco, in 2009, Riley tweeted: "Cisco just offered me a job! Now I have to weigh the utility of a fatty paycheck against the daily commute to San Jose and hating the work." Her tweet elicited a huge response on Twitter including from a Cisco associate who responded he'd be happy to pass her sentiments on to HR. Suffice it to say, her job offer disappeared.

Digital Footprint

How is your online presence? Anything you post on social media is public knowledge. It does not matter if it's your personal social media page, business page, company page, private page, or group page. They all represent your social media presence. Posting inappropriate information can adversely affect your professional career. I suggest to google your name and see how you are being represented online.

Benefits of Social Media

- Helps to grow your business or the company business
- Promotes interactions
- Builds relationships
- Increases sales
- Assists in getting your message out
- Builds your personal brand and image
- Opens doors of opportunities
- Expands your brand nationally and internationally

Email Etiquette

Email has practically replaced snail mail. It is more efficient for sending documents and letters all over the world. The amount of people you can communicate with through email is limitless. In the workplace, it is imperative that common courtesy and proper etiquette be practiced at all times to protect your image and that of the company.

Your Signature and Email Address

Your professional email address is like a handshake, the first introduction of yourself and your services. The email address that you select should make a first and lasting impression. Your email address should consist of your first and last name, or business name, with a reputable email service provider that says I'm serious about my reputation and professional image.

Voice Mail

A professional voicemail should include your name and your business name and begin with a warm greeting. It should make your prospects feel valued and welcome.

Respond to Emails Within 24 Hours

Professional etiquette requires that you respond to your emails within 24 hours. At least acknowledge that you received the email and will be getting back to them. Not responding in a timely manner is indicative of poor customer service.

Proper Protocol When Sending or Responding to Emails

Be respectful of others' time. Respond to emails during working hours to assure that the recipient receives your email or response. When responding after hours, you risk the recipient missing your email.

Writing Professional Emails

A professional email should include the subject line, salutation, body, ending, closing, and signature. The closing of your email should end with Thank you, Sincerely, or other appropriate closings. Read your correspondence for proper grammar, punctuation, and spelling before sending. Do not use emojis, text language, or slang language. Any business document you create will become a part of a permanent record and should always adhere to best business practices. Depending on the circumstance, your documents may be used in a court of law and should be accurate and professional.

The tone of your email should be written with caution, as you don't want to offend anyone. Never send an email using all caps. It indicates anger, screaming, or shouting. If you are upset, remain poised even in your writing. Avoid opening your personal email on your work computer. Legally, all emails opened on your work computer will become company property.

Chain Letters Emails in the Workplace

I strongly suggest that you refrain from sending those "good luck" or "God will bless you" chain letters. Chain letters are possibly linked to spam. On Facebook, chain letters were out of control to the point that I was requested to do a live session on social media etiquette. Everybody is not on Facebook for social purposes. Many on Facebook are users strictly for business purposes and would prefer interacting with potential clients only.

Sending Emails to a Group

Proper etiquette is to use a BCC (blind carbon copy) when sending to a group. This will prevent others from getting others' email address without permission. You don't want your email recipients to begin receiving unsolicited emails and spam from hundreds of people.

Risks versus Benefits of Exposing Too Much Information

Linda, an engineer in her early 30's, found herself jobless after her job decided after three months she was not a good fit. This sort of put Linda into a slump and affected her confidence. Linda and I had a few sessions to discuss her job aspirations. Linda began searching for jobs throughout the United States and was not having any luck. She persisted and finally landed four interviews in California, Tennessee, Houston, Carolina, and had several phone interviews. While on Facebook, I noticed Linda posted about her recent job interview in California and was excited about her next job interview in Tennessee. I recognized the issue with this and immediately contacted her to discuss the possible repercussions of her posting her itinerary of job interviews. I explained to her that one of the jobs may decide not to hire her if they discover she has possibly accepted a position from someone else. Another point to consider is the employer may move quickly to offer you the job because you will be a great asset. The risk is that you never know which way it may go, so why risk this type of exposure? After clarifying the risks and benefits, Linda thanked me and removed the post. She subsequently accepted a position in Houston as a Project Engineer.

Proper Technology Etiquette in the Workplace
- Do not wear earplugs in elevators or during business meetings
- Do not check your emails in an elevator
- Avoid having phone conversations while in an elevator
- Avoid checking your emails during face-to face conversations

The Art of Paper Correspondence

Paper correspondence still has its place in spite of computer and internet technology. Here are some tips on creating a professional document.

- Use a professional greeting such as "Dear" to set the tone of your business letter
- The use of Hi, Hello, or Hey are too casual and undermine your professionalism
- Avoid using fancy fonts
- Be consistent in formatting and style
- Use Mr. or Ms., To Whom It May Concern, Dear Sir or Madam, Dear Human Resource Manager, etc., if you do not know your contact's name
- Spell check everything before sending, especially names, titles, and company name
- Cross-reference by checking company website, calling the company, check business card, or check LinkedIn page
- For letter closings use Sincerely, Regards, Yours truly, and Yours Sincerely
- Beneath the closing, include your written signature and typed signature
- Include your contact information at the top and bottom beneath your typed signature

Set Yourself Apart with a Thank You Note

Professional thank you cards are a great way to be distinct and memorable. Sending thank you cards are also a great way to build relationships with business associates, referrals, and prospective clients.

- Thank you note cards can be handwritten or typed
- Thank you note cards are a way to show gratitude and should include what you are thankful for
- Send a thank you note card 24 hours after the encounter
- Thank you cards for personal gifts should be handwritten

Example Thank You Note

Professional Salutation

Dear Dr. Name,

Body of Thank You Note
1. Name specific appreciation
2. Benefits of gifts or deed
3. Reciprocate the favor

Thank you for meeting with me to discuss how I can improve my executive presence. You offered so much value and I am excited to get started on building my executive presence. I appreciate your assistance and I look forward to implementing the new strategies for my specific industry.

I'll be sure to send you a follow-up on my progress. Please let me know if and when I can return the favor.

Best regards,
Full Name

Closing
"Best regards"
"Sincerely"

Signature
1. Full name
2. Cursive writing

> "Set yourself apart as a business professional and show your gratitude by sending a "thank you" note card"
> ~ CAROLYN POWERY

The ladder.com surveyed 500 job seekers and hiring managers to get their opinion on the importance of sending thank you notes. Sixty-seven percent reported they send a thank you note after an interview. Forty-four percent said thank you cards are somewhat important and 32% said they were very, very important.

Key Point Summary

- A professional headshot is the first contact a potential business associate will have before a physical meeting

- An online professional presence conveys credibility and authority

- Always maintain professionalism and dignity on social media

- Never let trolls dictate your professional presence or make you argumentative

- Posting inappropriate information can adversely affect your professional career

- Your attitude is 90% of what people remember about you

- It is good etiquette to respond to emails within 24 hours

- Your professional email address is like a handshake, the first introduction of yourself and your services

- Your email address should consist of your first name and last name, or business name, with an appropriate email service provider that says I'm serious about my reputation and professional image

- A phone greeting should always convey value for the customer and be welcoming

- Send a handwritten thank you note to set yourself apart from the competition

The Essentials of Networking

Carolyn M. Powery

Do you exude executive presence at networking events? Is your executive presence setting you apart from the competition? Learn how to present your personal and professional brand in a way that exemplifies executive presence. Executive presence is the "It Factor" that causes others to gravitate towards you and want to know more about you. A study was conducted by the Center for Talent Innovation. After surveying 268 senior executives, it was reported that "executive presence" accounts for 26% of what it takes to be promoted.

> *"Your first 7 seconds of engagement with others will determine others perception of you and the trajectory of your career."*
> ~Carolyn Powery

Executive Presence
- Exudes gravitas
- Creates credibility
- Shows confidence
- Makes you appear more approachable
- Positions you as a leader
- Helps in marketing your services
- Promotes you as your brand
- Commands the room
- Builds trust and loyalty with your potential clients
- Conveys a poised, polished, professional personality

How can you benefit from networking?
- Opportunity to build long-lasting relationships
- Opportunity to connect with your ideal client
- Opportunity to serve others, not sell
- Increase your bottom line and revenue

Networking Faux Pas

I was invited to the Annual Marketing Conference for Aspiring Leaders. I decided to accept the invitation. This was an opportunity to advance my career. As I began to network, I saw the President of Mobile Phone Services. I saw this as the perfect opportunity to meet the President of this prestigious marketing company. As I walked in his direction, I summoned up the courage to introduce myself, but began to second-guess my expertise and wondered if I had what it took to work for a top marketing company. As I approached, my heart began to pound. I attempted to introduce myself with a plate in my left hand and a drink in my right hand. In that moment, I realized I committed a major faux pas. I was not able to make a positive first impression with a proper handshake. I was embarrassed. I just blew a once in a lifetime opportunity that potentially could have elevated my career to the next level.

Research conducted by the Carnegie Institute of Technology shows that 85% of your success in getting a promotion, advancing your career, increasing your revenue, or obtaining new clients is based on your people skills, and 15% is based on your technical knowledge. Nobel prize-winning Israeli-American psychologist, Daniel Kahneman, conducted another study. The results showed that people would rather do business with a person they like and trust rather than someone they do not.

How are your networking skills measuring up?

_____

_____

_____

_____

_____

_____

_____

What does executive presence have to do with networking?

The perception that others have of you will determine if others want to know more about you. Your personal and professional brand is essential in creating the executive presence you want to be known for. What do you want others to say about you when you are not in the room? Get strategic and create an image you want to project. To get started in taking your networking skills to the next level, master getting clarity on your ideal client, know your value, and get rid of the inner critic.

1. Get clarity
Knowing who your ideal clients are will help you to connect with:
- People who are your ideal clients
- People who know your ideal clients
- People who do business with your ideal clients

When you identify your ideal clients, it will help you to be crystal clear on who you serve and prevent you from wasting time with someone who is not your ideal client. Networking opportunities can be formal or informal settings. Informal meetings can occur in the form of a conference, lunch, seminars, and receptions. Take advantage of these opportunities and be ready to give a positive first impression. It takes less than 7 seconds to make a positive first impression and you will not be given a second chance.

2. Know your value
Answering the following questions will help you to make a positive first impression. Once you have completed this assessment, you will have more clarity on which networking events are suitable and worth your time.

How will I offer value? _____
_____
_____
_____
_____

How will this particular networking event benefit me? _____
_____
_____
_____
_____
_____

Effective networking is the lifeline of your business. Networking represents an opportunity to make valuable connections and should not be treated like speed dating. As a professional, networking properly is a must in order for your business or career to be sustained. Not too long ago the only way professionals connected was face to face. There were no computers or social media. Networking relied solely on face-to-face interactions.

3. Identify your inner critic

Is it possible that you could be sabotaging your networking opportunities before you show up at the event? Your executive presence should exude confidence when others encounter you. Do you see networking events as a waste of time? Do you believe they are effective? Are you fearful of what others think? Do you believe you are a leader?

Imagine arriving at a networking event, walking into a roomful of people you have not had the pleasure of meeting. You begin to feel out of place. Fear sets in and you begin to question your professional ability. Self-limiting beliefs begin to deflate your confidence and negative thoughts begin to surface. You wonder if anyone will be interested in your services. Because networking is unpredictable, it is important to begin with a positive mindset. If you think positive, you will attract positive. If you think negative, you will attract negative. Visualize yourself as a connector, influencer, leader, and someone whom others want to connect with.

Public speaking is the number one fear that most people experience. I conducted a survey on various social media websites to get an idea of the challenges that entrepreneurs and professionals have with networking. Below are some of the networking challenges professionals encounter.

- Tending to freeze up
- Feeling more comfortable with one-on-one interactions
- Approaching new and unfamiliar people
- Figuring out how to start an appropriate conversation

Tips to Network with Influence

What is my role at a networking event? Your goal at a networking event is to connect, build relationships, offer value to the conversation, and be the solution to someone's problem. The quickest way to be tuned out is to approach with the intent to sell and not serve. "You can have everything in life you want if you will just help other people get what they want," Zig Ziglar.

Be prepared and do your research. Now that you have the mindset, prepare for the networking event. Before attending a networking event, you need to have a plan. Treat a networking event the same as if you were preparing for a job interview or presenting for a million dollar contract. Implement the following strategies.

- Identify at least three people you wish to connect with at the event and research them
- Visit the company website and familiarize yourself with projects and future projects
- Google and familiarize yourself with their industry
- Talk about their interests, alma mater, and hobbies
- Be knowledgeable about current events
- Focus on the potential client and not yourself
- Have a 10-30 seconds elevator speech

Note: One connection can change the trajectory of your business or career. Dress to Impress! Dress the way you want to be addressed or dress for the job you want. Dressing in casual or nightlife attire in a professional setting will cause you to immediately lose credibility. Your appearance should be professional and polished.

Maximize your networking time. If you are looking to connect with the CEO or President, arrive on time. You will have a 30-minute window of opportunity to connect with key people due to their busy schedules. It is imperative that you arrive on time to give yourself a better opportunity to meet the decision makers of the organization. Spend a maximum of 10 minutes with each person. To maximize your time spend 80% of your time listening and 20% talking.

Gracefully Enter and Exit a Group. Walk into the room with confidence and step to the right side of the door entrance. Discreetly scan the room to see who you think you would like to connect with. Remember that others are doing the same thing, so stand up straight, smile, and put your best foot forward. To end a conversation graciously, simply say, "It was a pleasure meeting you, perhaps we could have lunch in the near future," and depart.

Comfortably Network and Mingle with Strangers. To effectively master mingling with strangers, it is key that you understand the dynamics of groups of people before approaching during a networking event. You should decide whether the the groups are open or closed.

A person standing alone is the quickest way to connect. The easiest groups of people to approach are open groups of two to three people. An open group has an opening where the individuals are looking outward and not facing each other head on. Closed groups of two, three, or four people forming a circle are harder to penetrate.

Introduce Yourself with a Firm Handshake. Approach with a smile, extend a firm, confident handshake, and make eye contact as you give your full name and title. Gender is irrelevant when introducing yourself in the business arena. If you want to be seen as having executive presence, boldness and confidence, extend your hand first. Always stand when there is an introduction. Maintain eye contact 60% of the time when conversing. If making eye contact is uncomfortable, look at the person's eyebrows or mouth.

Introduction example: My name is Carolyn Powery and I am the CEO and Founder of Prestige Etiquette and Image Consulting. I help professionals and entrepreneurs set themselves apart, outclass the competition and gain a competitive edge that monetizes. Recently, I helped a client increase her level of confidence by securing her dream job after being dismissed from her job. I wrote an article called "A Polished Professional" to help professionals maximize their executive presence. I would love to share it with you, I think you will find it of value.

Business Introduction Protocol When Introducing Others

The highest ranking or most important person should be introduced first. Determine who is the VIP (Very Important Person) during an introduction. There is one exception. The client will be the VIP in introductions. In the business world, women are always addressed as Ms. when the marital status is unknown and males use Mr. in front of their last name.

Introducing others example:
1. Mr. or Ms. VIP, I would like to introduce Mr. or Ms. Lesser VIP.
2. Angela Snow (client), this is Cody Smith, our company's CEO. Cody Smith, this is Angela Snow, our client from Texas World Class Corporation.

During an introduction, if you have common knowledge that both parties share, make it part of your additional information introduction. Example, they both have graduated from the same university.

Name Tag Etiquette

The proper way to display your name tag on your clothing is 4 inches below your right shoulder. This will automatically guide your gaze up the right arm to the name tag while simultaneously giving a firm handshake. Your full name should be written on the name tag along with your title.

Ways to Remember Names

- Repeat the person's name
- Associate the name with someone famous, a family member, or friend
- Visualize seeing the person's name in print on a business card
- Ask to repeat name if name is difficult to pronounce

Proper Business Card Protocol

A first impression is a lasting impression. It takes six seconds for an individual to form an opinion. Which of the following shows that you are a true, organized, and a serious professional when presenting your business cards?

1. Business cards in your back pocket
2. Business cards in a zip-lock bag
3. Business cards in a business card holder
4. Business cards with a rubber band around them

Put your best foot forward by presenting clean crisp business cards in a slim business card holder. Image is everything. Avoid presenting business cards wrapped with rubber bands or from your back pocket. Business cards are a snapshot of the way you conduct your affairs. Always present your business cards facing the other person. Keep your business cards in pristine condition and keep them safeguarded.

Business Card Exchange Etiquette

Maintain professionalism when exchanging business cards and avoid being aggressive in giving out your business cards. When offering your business cards, wait until you have had a conversation and established rapport with the person before offering your business card. Show courtesy by reading the person's business card before putting it away. Business cards are also a great conversation starter. Never ask for a person's card of higher status (more than one level above your position). You should wait for the person to offer his or her card. If you should meet the CEO or top executive, never ask for their card. If they show an interest in you, extend your business card with the hope that they will offer their business card.

Successful Approach to Small Talk

Be prepared ahead of time. Acquire knowledge to be able to ask business-related questions or discuss current events. The main focus should be on the person you are engaging small talk with, not on you. Plan to talk to at least three new people and obtain new pieces of information. Also, have your 1-30 seconds elevator speech.

Great business-related questions are:
- Who would you choose if I could connect you with an ideal client?
- How did you get started in this business?
- What tools are you using to brand your image?
- What separates your company from your competition?
- What do you foresee as new trends in your business?

How to Finesse Eating and Greeting at a Networking Event

The food at a networking event is not in place of dinner. The main reason for attending a networking event is to make connections. The best practice is to eat before arriving so your focus is not on the cuisine. If you choose to eat at a networking event, keep your right hand free for handshakes and use your left hand to eat and drink.

Do not:
- Pass out business cards to everyone in the room as if it's a poker game
- Solicit business cards
- Be obnoxious, loud, and boisterous
- Monopolize the conversation to make yourself look important
- Rudely cut people off during the conversation
- Hang around the food table eating and drinking

The Power of Follow-Up

The contacts you make networking will not cultivate a relationship on their own. It will require some additional follow-up such as a phone call or thank you note. Nurture your new relationships and do something to stand out from all the other networkers. Start with sending a little thank you card, something that will make your new contacts smile, remember you, and make you stand out from the crowd. Continue developing the relationship with a phone call and set up a meeting over coffee or lunch. If you know of an event that will be of interest to your new connection, let them know about it. If you should come across an article that relates to your new business connection, send a copy of the article with a short note.

> *"The way you communicate, dress, and present yourself, will determine what you attract and how others perceive you."*
> ~CAROLYN POWERY

Body Language

Leona Johnson

These are just a few common gestures that can help you understand different body languages. Body language, no matter which way you use it, whether it's your head, your mouth or your eyes, it all has a meaning to help you understand each gesture. The general study of body language is **Kinesics**. It is used to easily interpret what body communications like facial expressions and gestures mean. An example would be the study of body posture. Your body sends messages about yourself and your confidence. Your signal shows "I dominate" when you walk in. Great posture is having your head high, totally owning the room. Closed body language signal is having your head down, no eye contact and no confidence about yourself, displaying "I don't want to be social." All the movements generated by the body is how we understand body language.

Body language is a form of nonverbal communication in which information is exchanged without using words. Some examples include but are not limited to: blinking, eye rolling, playing with your hair, foot tapping, and leaning in. All of these actions will send messages to the person with whom you are conversing with. The ability to read other people's body language is a highly sophisticated skill. According to researchers, "Body language accounts for about 50 to 70% of our communication. Body language uses nonverbal techniques to relay messages seen through your expressions of feelings, thoughts, intentions and physical behavior." There are plenty of ways to communicate, but body language is known to be the most highly effective.

This form of communication easily lets the other person understand your thoughts and feelings by your actions alone.

Body language is also a two-way form of communication. Firstly, other people understand the real meanings of how you feel and secondly, you get to understand true meaning of others' feelings. This happens on both the conscious and subconscious level of the mind. For you to communicate effectively, it is important that you have an understanding of body language. However, it is also important that you understand some other signals that will help you through the process.

Poised Polished Professional

As a professional, it is very important that you do not send the wrong message to your clients, colleagues, or business associates. Body language and nonverbal cues can come across wrong and get completely mixed up. For instance, let's say you've prepared for an interview and upon arrival, you are asked to have a seat at a desk in front of the interviewer. The interviewer notices right away that you are shaking and tapping your foot from the moment you sit down. At this point, she is annoyed but she continues her questioning. At the same time, she is trying to analyze which signal you are sending and asks the question "Are you nervous?" Tapping can mean many things. It could mean one has anxiety or is impatient. It could also mean you are in a hurry or it could mean that you are just thinking. But most of all, it can mean you are not aware of the body languages you display. It is very important to eliminate these behaviors as soon as possible, or it will cause you to become irritated, lose focus during the interview, and it can also cost you the job. My advice to you would be to learn breathing techniques that will calm you down before an interview or meeting. Get there early so you have enough time to calm your nerves and not show early signals of negative body languages.

Another example may be when you're having conversations with colleagues at an event. In this case, you should try eliminating non-verbal noises like fixing and adjusting your ties when you are talking, pulling at your clothes, or adjusting your watch constantly. All of these things make noises and are inappropriate non-verbal body languages. People pick up on these signs and it will always cause a pause or interruptions during the conversation. In contrast, suppose you're at the same corporate event and you are meeting the owner of a prestigious law firm. You should always look him in the eye extend a handshake with confidence and say, "It's a pleasure to meet you, Mr./Mrs. _____, I am _____." This will convey the message of security, honesty and confidence. You can also say, "Mr. Jones, I would like to introduce myself. My name is _____." with an extended hand. Try it when you're at a corporate event and see what difference it will make when your body language displays confidence and reassurance.

Body language cues have great impact when we are interacting with others, it gives us power to hurt people's feelings without saying any words, so you have to be very careful on how you express what you want to say without offending other people. It is very important to learn other signals that will help you through the body language process.

Here are some examples for body languages:

Eyes- There is an old saying that goes "Your eyes are the window to your soul." I heard that as a child and as I got older, I understood this through body language. Your eyes are one of the best tools for body language that help you understand interpersonal communication.

When you are talking to other people, you have to maintain eye contact so that the person you are speaking with understands that you are paying close attention to what they were saying. When you are talking to a group of people, try making eye contact with each and every person rather than one person. Therefore, they will understand you are talking to everyone in the group. It also communicates a lot when you avoid direct eye contact with other people, as it can come across as not being truthful, not really interested in talking, or that you are shy. Other eye body languages can be eye gazing, roaming eyes, rolling eyes, your pupil size, and blinking.

Facial- Facial expression shows a lot of emotions. It indicates a lot of what you are feeling and how you are thinking. A smile is a great example of body language. Smiling indicates happiness, joy, excitement and grace. A smile can light up someone's day because it displays energetic nonverbal signals. Each of these interpret a positive message. The term "tears of joy" shows signs of happiness and sadness through emotions. Frowning can express anger, frustration, or even confusion. We need to

Legs, hands and arms- You can send important messages with your leg, hand, and arm movements through body language. Waving is a sign that displays hello or goodbye. A fist tap means "cool" or okay; but a balled up fist can mean a fight signal. Two fingers up mean peace or deuces. Thumbs up means great job; or it can mean okay or cool. Hands placed together can display position for prayer or a grateful gesture. I am actually guilty of conveying the wrong message through body language. I used to talk to people and stand in front of them with my arms crossed, it became habit. It was not until someone I knew very well told me that I was indicating poor body language. I was told crossing my arms meant I was being protective of myself or that I really did not want to be there or talk to the person. So, it is very common to use some body language even as a child and not understand the meaning. However, the most common would be teenagers. They are quick to hold their arms up & across the chest; it can be very offensive to parents. It definitely indicates you do not want to hear it or are being defensive. Another sign is when a person clasps their hands behind them. This often indicates boredom, being anxious or impatient. Now, good posture that expresses itself positively means knees together, legs together, and feet flat. You should never cross your legs. Crossing your legs can send a message that you need privacy.

Mouth- Movements of the mouth helps you understand body language. Lips tell a lot of stories. Puckered lips can indicate a kiss or a frown indicating your sorry. Putting your hands over your mouth can mean "oops, I made a mistake" or "let me shut up" or "I'm sorry". Biting the lip can mean you are nervous or angry or Biting the lip can indicate insecurity or nervousness; or when flirting, " I like you".

The type of body language communicated through body positioning is called **Proxemics.** This communication is the personal space aspect of body language. This space is in a area where people are trusted more like gathering with friends and family. Here is where you would experience public communicating like addressing others and having personal and casual conversations. The Social side of communication would be family gatherings, consulting with others, and intimate gatherings as well. In each of these situations, the distance kept will continue varying. I found that when you are able to read other people's body language, you can understand their feelings, what they really mean and what they really want to say. Understanding body language will help improve your relationships in a better way; for example, knowing what others feel and what they mean. In order for that to happen, you have to have emotional intelligence to determine and understand the feelings of others. You will never make the mistake of doing something that goes contrary to what others feel when you understand the signs. You have to practice it. Everyone has the skills for this type of communication, but if you practice regularly, you will perfect the act of reading people's body language as a professional. You will learn how to understand non verbal signals and how to perceive them.

Nonverbal signals may be interpreted differently by others, which in some cases, may lead to misunderstandings. Most times people will not have the confidence to tell you how they are feeling from word-of-mouth and you are most likely get it through their nonverbal actions like a huge sigh or twisting mouth or lips. Imagine someone not accommodating you when you are close to them or not talking to you while sitting by you; it may be a sign that a person does not allow others in their personal space. When you are talking to someone and they shift their eyes in the opposite way, it can be assumed that they don't like what you are saying. However, these are normal body language reactions that play a vital role in our lives because they show how other people perceive of your actions without conversing verbally. The purpose of knowing and understanding body language is that it is another option for expressing our feelings. It feels safer to express body language if it is understood by a person rather than spoken language because spoken language can really be complex. For example, verbal communication could involve having a friend that you never want to talk to but you're forced to face this person and express this to his/her face. It may be difficult to say "I don't want to see you again." Ouch, that hurts. A nonverbal expression could be just simply ignoring this person & never answering calls. This will eventually lead to he/she understanding that you do not want them around.

Body language for men and women can be different. We often use body language to show affection to the opposite sex and/or the lack of it through non verbal communication. For example, my favorite form of body language is flirting. It can be very productive & in most cases can get you results. This type of body language captures the opposite sex more than talking will do. The most common example of this is a wink or eye contact. A man may gesture for a woman to come to him by a wave or nodding the head to the side. This is an unspoken connection between two people. Most women flirt when they know a man is looking by walking past him with confidence, swishing, their head high, nice posture or they may even run their fingers through their hair or place it behind their ear in a flirty way during the initial eye contact.

Men and women deal with communication differently. It is typical for women to express their feelings both verbally and nonverbally while it is a characteristic for men to be less emotionally expressive. For instance, it is socially acceptable for girls to cry silently and openly while boys are told to behave like men and not to cry like a girl; that's when they breath in and out from the chest silently to hold in the tears. When a woman nods during a conversation it usually means "I understand what you were saying". When a man nods in a discussion it means "I agree with you.". Women normally use more facial expressions than men. For example, some women smile more when interacting with people in a social setting. Women interpret body language better than men. Researchers argue that women have the "female intuition "and innate ability which allows them to read body language better than men. Women who have raised a child has a better intuition due to a special personal bond between mom and child. During a child's early years, women learn how to rely completely on body language. Women display nurturing behaviors, show more emotions and the feelings come through by displaying various body language. Women tend to do better at receiving messages, especially when it comes to noticing inconsistency in between body language and verbal language. Men tend to be less skilled at using subtle body languages to influence communication without seeming to be doing so at all. When most women are angry, they shut down and display anger silently. Men use nonverbal body language like anger and hostile behaviors in order to hide his feelings like pain and fear, which are associated with failure, weakness and emotions. These are things that are understandable in some stereotypical men. Understanding of differences in language can help a great deal in preventing misinterpretations of body languages. When these differences occur, it will be easier to resolve potential conflicts and misunderstandings as it relates to verbal and nonverbal body language.

Dealing With Difficult People

LEONA JOHNSON

Dealing with difficult people can cause many different types of distractions and/or confrontations in the workplace. This is not something that the average employee wants to deal with in the workplace or as a professional. What are your thoughts as a professional when you are put in a situation where you have to deal with difficult people? As professionals, what are some ways that we can redirect the attack and communicate with our peers ending with a greater impact? Well, first, you have to understand the importance of social skills. Social skills consists of but is not limited to, being poised, polished and polite; great social skills involve walking away if the situation gets difficult. However, redefined social skills include mastery of all forms of interpersonal communication. A polished, well socialized person must be able to communicate one on one as well as in groups. An impactful communicator can think on his feet, read a room, negotiate effectively, avoid alterations, actively listen and create value and opportunity. We must use social skills to to demonstrate respect towards others and exhibit integrity.

Most successful people have well rounded social skills that range from table manners and grooming to communication. Learn and practice the skills of communicating with others, and it will become second nature. For example, an articulate person who speaks rudely or gruffly while demonstrating perfect table manners will not be remembered for the way he held his fork. In all likelihood, his dining companion walks away from the meal thinking about how embarrassing and uncomfortable it was to dine with someone who spoke rudely to the waiter and went on and on about himself for the whole meal. Basic rules of decency demands that we act civilly towards each other, and that means being polite even to those people that you don't like that much. It is difficult to have a conversation with someone, join a group, or give a speech when you get a prickly reception. For example, if you are in a meeting and went to greet a person and you are ignored, or if someone shows disinterest while turning her back and looking down at her phone, would you want to have a conversation or pursue that person to be your friend or coworker?

There are four primary reasons as to why social skills are important:

1) To put people at ease and help them feel comfortable, 2) To help demonstrate respect for others and for ourselves, 3) To show we value others, and 4) To exhibit integrity, honesty, and authenticity. Although you will not like everyone you come across, especially difficult people, social skills guidelines state that even if you do not like someone, you can still behave civilly, courteously, and politely. It is also possible to treat people with dignity and respect even if you are not socially comfortable. Aside from the workplace, difficult and problematic people may be in your family, at school, at church, or anywhere else that is a social setting. Quite frankly, dealing with these types of situations can be very draining. Fortunately, there is hope. There are several search strategies that help deal with different types of difficult people; these apply to even the worst types of bullies in the workplace. I will first give you examples of difficult office types.

#1. The needy one (man or woman): This person has the most difficulty with managing their social skills. The needy person requires constant refueling and validation. This person will always feel worthless. The needy person will go out their way to get any kind of social feedback or acceptance from their peers.It is almost like dealing with a preschool-aged child. Their own actions are the sole reason they whine and complain so much to others. This difficult type of behavior will eventually either lead to the Mr./Mrs/ Independent personality or the worst of all, the terminator. These types of people will go to great lows to achieve their own success. They will lie, cheat or even steal others ideas and/or success (if it was necessary) to remind the world constantly of their new achievement(s). They have no conscience. Eventually, his or her neediness will transform into anger and hostility against the people who do not give them affection, sending him or her to act on revenge.

#2. Mr or Mrs Paranoid: This personality type is constantly screaming "No one in the office respects me! Everybody in the office is always mad and out to get me!" This type of co-workers will take offense to any and everything you do. This difficult type of personality will yell & be very offensive. They also will not hesitate to tell you anything about yourself but cannot take anything you tell them. This person will have more enemies than allies but they will never recognize that the problem is them and not the people around them. This person is constantly angry, bringing personal issues to work and is mad at the world. This person is very hostile and makes it very difficult for anyone to work with them.

#3. Mr./Mrs. Independent: In the office, this personality is Misses or Mister know it all. They are very arrogant and live above and beyond the normal standard of society when they walk in the room. They want and have to to be seen. If you are not talking about him or her, the topic will swing shift over quickly. He or she acts as the givers of advice as if they know everything; they think they know the truth about everything no matter what situation you are in. Mr./Mrs. Independent, as I mentioned previously, had been formerly the needy guy. By contrast, Mr./Mrs. Independent appears to be unaffected by the need of approval. He or she says and does whatever they like without caring how others feel. He or she will take all the paper out of your printer to use without asking. When they are approached about it, they make it very difficult to own up to their wrongdoings.

#4. The bulldozer(bully): He/she actually gets mental and physical pleasure from hurting others. They feel no wrongdoing when they screw somebody over to achieve their own goals. They normally take pleasure in hurting others because it makes them feel stronger. The bully normally holds a position in middle management of most companies. However, you will less likely see that they make upper management. In fact, most people in upper management has a bad opinion about the bully. They may say something like "Oh, Who? Mason? Yes, he's great at getting numbers but he's just not a people person and you probably will not see him make upper management anytime soon." See, that's a classic example of sabotage. The bully is the worker that yells at someone if they are not making their numbers in front of others. To the bully, this dominance makes them feel bigger and the person less; he/ she gets a thrill from that.

#5. The terminator: Finally, the worst of all the problems or issues in the workplace. This person displays passive aggressiveness, regardless of where they are and who they are with. This personality type appears to be nice, pleasant and easy to get along with… on the outside. However, on the inside, they have a vengeance and hatred against you. The scary part is that they understand that in the web of others, they have to be fake, smile and be a chamaeleon. They also may be difficult to work with and sabotage your work to get you fired based on nothing more than jealousy and envy. They will get you in a cunning way so good that the terminator may even be assessing you. You can identify the terminator by the reputation they have. The terminator personality type will try to sabotage other workers' opportunities in any way possible. These types of people may try to downplay others to make themselves look good. For example, a conversation between a new employee Jan and the terminator personality type may go similar to this: "I want to work with Austin the next week on the new project. He's ahead of everyone else on the team and he's nice." says Jan. "Oh, well um.. you may want to be careful of Austin." "Well, why?", Jan replies. "He gets projects that others are supposed to start. Just last year he took a project from Dan, who was fired because his wife stole the portfolio and claimed she lost it and Austin found out about it and that's why Dan got fired." Jan says, "Ohhh... well, okay." Most terminators are difficult people to work with. They are shrewd and downright evil. They prey upon the weak, especially to move ahead and up the ladder.

It is possible that in your profession you have a will be dealing with these difficult types. In fact, you may be one of these people and if so, instead of labeling them difficult people take a moment and think about the role you play in your own social interactions. Once you recognize it, adjust your behavior so that you will not have any hostile feelings towards others to create a better atmosphere. You must free yourself and improve yourself, staying poised and polished.

Strategies for dealing with these types of difficult people: (#1) There are great reasons to believe there is a good person inside of every difficult person. You have to be more professional one to bring out the best in each one of you. (#2) There will be times you find yourself with proof personalities affect the entire team that's one upper management has step in to keep that person in check. For the bullies with the terminator, you may have to gather evidence until have enough to move forward. Outsmart them and use it so that when they try to screw anyone over, you will catch them on it. You must document everything. I doubt if they try to sabotage anyone else. No one wants their job threatened. Do not be afraid to take action! Remember that no single strategy will adequately help every person and you will never fully understand any individual. However, never let the ignorance or rudeness of someone else be a distraction to you. Always communicate with others with respect and dignity.

It is important to realize that not everyone will gravitate to your happiness. In fact, some people are on a mission to make us miserable in the office setting. There is always one person who loves to hijack others happiness. Do not be alarmed. You can not change how that person reacts, you can only change your own reactions. When working with coworkers, colleagues or business partners, for success, your interaction has to be effective with each person. You have to go right into problem-solving mode so you can stand up to others without fighting. With each person it will be handled differently but it has to be effective. Examples of difficult situations can be: noise in the office, talking too loud on the phone, socializing and just simply hovering around one's cubicle. There is also eating smelly food at your desk, gossiping or just being plain out obnoxious. However, there are several ways that these situations can be handled.

First, you have to come up with a strategy in which you can be kind and respect others in a tactful way. Most companies have a human resource department that handles these types of situations. However, in many cases, most coworkers are comfortable enough to handle it on their own. Examples would be: having private conversations, making polite requests, or even creating a company policy to change behaviors. Another more hands on example would be saying "It has come to my attention that the noise is a little distracting on the floor and if you would be so kind to lower your voices while others are on the phone. I would appreciate that and thank you for understanding." Rudeness can be viewed in different ways. Sometimes it is not what you say, but how you say it. Now, there is blatant rudeness as in, just coughing without covering my mouth. Then, there is also rudeness that is more insidious; rudeness that we sometimes run into in the office and business situations. When we act ill mannered or insensitive, we make people feel unhappy, uncomfortable or uneasy. Etiquette is all about putting people at ease. In business, it is important to get a grasp of unkindness and what it means to cause others discomfort. The best way to deal with difficult people is to act politely.

Office etiquette example: You walk away from the copier to grab your water. When you return, a co worker is standing there getting ready to use the copier but you are not quite done and your papers are still printing. You say "Hello, Nancy, I'm not sure if you realize this but, I was using this copier and I'm not quite finished yet; but the office down the hall has a new copier and it's open for use now." If you use a proper and polite response, most coworkers will recognize their mistake and adjust their behavior. Nancy will probably apologize and quickly move to the next office. Now, what if Nancy happens to be very rude? Well, you can still use text tactful behavior and discretion. For instance, what if Nancy is acting unkind and she says, "No, I don't like that copier because it runs too slow! I want to use this one. Plus, it will only take a second.", with no consideration that you were there first. You may question yourself and sigh. You ask yourself "Are getting these copies done that important? Is this a battle I want to fight?" Always take time to consider your response. Let Nancy use the copier. Alternatively, you can let it go and remember that it would not make a big difference in your day. Most likely, you will not even see her again because it is the end of the day. It is not polite to get hot and bothered, to argue or fight a rude and difficult person. 99% of the time it's not worth it. It is always just best to walk away, because most often in business you going to run into more business situations with people who are rude and difficult. Bottom line, it is better for your career to just to avoid being labeled as being the person to fight for every situation to prove a point. All in all, regardless you must always stay poised, polished and professional.

Poised Polished Professional

THE EXPERTS' GUIDE TO EXECUTIVE PRESENCE

PART IV
PILLAR 3- APPEARANCE GROOMING POSTURE

Models Attorney Neal White, Gina White, Actress
Photos courtesy of Teddy

Poised Polished Professional

PART IV
PILLAR 3- APPEARANCE GROOMING POSTURE

Grooming Posture
Leona Johnson

Posture is the position in which we hold our bodies while standing, sitting or lying down. Good posture is the correct alignment of body parts. Without posture and the muscles that control it, we would simply just fall to the ground. Good posture is the proper alignment from our head shoulders and pelvic. Pelvic posture is also known as the comparative position, these are parts of the body that are resting or doing movement. If a person has rounded shoulders while standing this is typically caused by poor postural habits, muscles unbalanced, and this person may focus too much on one type of exercise. Lots of people focus on strength when they exercise meanwhile, they are neglecting the upper back exercises that strengthens the core, focusing on upper back and chest muscles will help correct rounded shoulders. When you have a pain in your neck and it's not caused by trauma posture can be a contributing factor. Learn to identify the cause and have it properly corrected.

Correct posture gives you grace. If you walk in a room and you are properly dressed, you walk with grace and your presence is known, this is an essential part of a well-groomed person. For this to happen one must walk straight, stand tall, no hunching or slouching. Your body must be upright and relaxed. Your hands look better when they hang down to your sides. A graceful posture lies in a woman's appeal it's refined as a pleasure to see, it's very flattering and speaks volumes of your confident ways. The characteristics of correct body posture is that which comes with enthusiasm, confident, alertness and well-being. Personality and manners reflect the body language of any person. Poor posture impedes energy flow, a negative impact, mentally, physically and spiritually growth. Conversely, good posture will also help improve one's physical spiritual and mental state of being. According to European and particularly Parisian standards of sitting etiquette, the lady must never cross her legs in public. You may have noticed film stars do that, but the European protocol repudiates the method of sitting that way as distasteful. This is because when you sit like that, you may give the indication that you are fatigue, and therefore clumsy.

Ladies simply always keep your knees and your ankles together while sitting. Keep your soles on the floor while the heels remain at work. This will flatter your legs too, without transgressing the limits of decency. Educated, articulate women always keep the knees and ankles together, never cross your legs in public. You're a lady not an entertainer. I can remember when I was 12 my grandmother was always telling me to sit up in my chair and not to slouch when I stood. "Stand tall," I remember her saying, "you'll thank me later". I really didn't understand the importance of it, but I wanted to make her happy, so I started reading books about Royals- kings and queens and the lifestyle they live and that was the first Etiquette teaching I had for myself. I wanted to surprise my grandmother (Cleora) so I grabbed books the old-fashioned way to learn proper posture. I sat with my back against the chair in the upright position practicing everywhere I went. (I still sit with my bottom torso rest against any chair). I positioned books on my head to walk straight. I did it over and over, books falling everywhere, until I finally made it across the room. I was amused to say the least, at the thought of why I was doing this to myself. After all, grandma didn't even know I was working so hard.

That's when I took a liking to the Royal lifestyle. I studied them and learned all about the courts and I'm still a fan of the Royals. I still love the pearls, hats, and broaches and tea parties. The next time my grandmother saw me, I was too excited to show her what I had read, executed, and learned in three weeks. We were both avid readers, so she wasn't as surprised as she was proud. It felt like I had won an award because the irony of it is, she made me feel that way. There was no turning back I had to display good manners and etiquette around grandma all the time. She knew I took pride in learning about it for her and I almost felt ashamed as I grew older if I didn't display what I was determined to learn in her presence. Yes, at twelve, I read books about etiquette sitting and standing and the importance of posture.

I still read those books and I even studied the English standard in which they have tea parties and how to conduct them. I got a new tea party set that year for the holiday and I would make my brothers fake tea and pretend to have parties (they didn't like it) but my sisters would play with me and they never took me seriously. I really thought I was creating the ambiance of the elite, I dressed up and everything. (Ha ha) No one nor myself anticipated I was destined and that grandma groomed me for my passion of etiquette, manners, protocol, and civility today. Once I started studying for my Certifications it came easy. My readings became my understandings and why my I'm so passionate about civility. I take pride in helping others understand the importance of etiquette through my training and learning experiences.

With good posture, standing tall is considered the most important leadership signal, no matter where and what type of environment we work in. Good posture-shoulders, back straight, and planted feet reflects grace, confidence and authority. Slap torso, shifty eyes or shifty feet displays lack of energy and respect. Elegance is something that you can achieve, even if you're not born with it, it takes determination and practice always practice and always be poised polished and professional. Grooming-taking care of one's body it requires cleansing of your body parts taken care of the sense organs and wary of clean and comfortable clothing. Grooming focuses on the general cleaning, neatness & appearance. Grooming is a part of hygiene and image projection.

Why is good grooming important? You must have self-respect and consideration for the feelings of others. It's important to be self-aware and always looking out for hygiene problems, body odor, bad breath, greasy hair, dandruff, dirty nails, and any problems. Men should always be groomed facial hair cut nose and ear hair trimmed, no matter the style of the men's cut, it's important not to have shabby stubble facial hair that is uncapped. Shower daily, brush your teeth twice a day, use antiperspirant to stay looking clean and smelling fresh, finally always get enough sleep so that you don't look tired and haggard. Being professional requires being well groomed. Looking polished or put together is the most important physical asset of professionals. According to (CTI) researcher's women are judged more harshly than men. Well 83% of senior executives, said, "unkept attire" wrinkled or too tight clothing or visible lingerie detracts from a woman's executive presence. A slider smaller percentage 76% said it undermines a man's.

Moreover, women's professional polish includes tasteful accessories, manicure nails in a hairstyle versus a haircut. Whereas a man's polish look is based on a clean nail, shining shoes, a clean shave, a manicure and facial hair. There are companies that have rules about grooming, such as facial hair for men. These companies can tell them how long or how short they can wear their hair. The length of hair should not exceed the color of the shirt. In most cases if you sign a contract that they have about facial hair or length you must follow those rules. However, if you decide not to work there, that's your choice. But by signing the contract it says, I want to work here.

Dress code -many employers also require their employees to follow a dress code. These dress clothes are legal if they are not discriminatory. Men and women can have different dress codes if the dress codes do not put an unfair burden on one gender. Discrimination dress grooming policies may violate Title V11 of the Civil Rights Act 1964. Dressing for success includes a lot more than choosing the right outfit. To complete your look, you must consider accessories and personal grooming. How you present yourself to others can make or break a job interview or even cautious of a promotion at work. Your appearance is your employer's appearance. That is, how you present yourself at work is a direct reflection on your employer as well. A man should wear business suits in basic colors, keep your pockets, empty and avoid tinkling coins or keys or bulges. Avoid candy and chewing gum in meetings. Use portfolio case or briefcase for documents do not use folders in between your arms. Some people have personal flares for styles, but if it doesn't fit into the conservative or the corporate environment you may need to adapt.

A woman's professional appearance should support her accomplishments not show off the wrong assets. Avoid clothes that are revealing. Dresses should be proper length. My advice- know the dress code of your employer. Hairstyle should be neat and conservative, preferably off the face the color should not be harsh or an unusual hair color, it should be neatly and nicely brushed. Hair should be regularly trimmed to not lose its style manageability. Untied hair should not cover any part of your face (e.g. eyes) neatly and in place. Keep your makeup simple and appropriate for daytime. Keep it minimum and natural with neutral shades. Wearing no makeup can be as bad as wearing too much. Limit your jewelry. Bangles, loud and large jewelry are discouraged, no anklets.

Do not let your scent preferences be the first impression about yourself avoid wearing heavy scented colognes and perfumes. It may be your favorite, but it has no place overtaken business environment. Wearing heavy scented perfume/cologne can trigger, asthma, overpower room and often be offensive more often than pleasing. Many businesses are smoke-free but many are scents free. Even if you're a smoker and you smoke in your car your clothing will pick up that sent. Smokers should take care to avoid nicotine stains on the teeth and hands as well as tobacco breath ensure before you get within your areas of work you get rid of smells. If you were interviewing for a job the smell kept the interviewer from focusing on your skills.

Demonstrating personal grooming shows that you care about your personal appearance. Lastly body piercings and tattoos. They are very trendy, but not judged fondly amongst business professionals. Most people feel they are an expression of free will being themselves. But when it comes to your career & other people's' feelings I strongly feel you should think on whether you decide to get a piercing or a tattoo that displays unprofessionalism. There are some decisions we make in life that will have repercussions in your professional career. Some corporate Businesses in the US has strict policies against visible tattoos and piercing in the workplace. In some cases, it hinders a person's career. In corporate America judgment still exist about tattoos. The prejudices may be judgmental as biased, but you must understand the impact they may potentially have on your career opportunities. Even when we make decisions in our early 20s to leave a visual permanent tattoo and piercings, it can affect our chances later in life of moving to a job that we dreamed of when we are in our 30s and up. Tattoos are not protected by the First Amendment (freedom expression), corporate can discriminate against the professional. Many corporations band visible tattoos and piercings. They have that right according to equal employment opportunity commission (EEOC) your image in professional corporate Jobs requires great grooming.

What can you do to add that extra leverage in your grooming for your dream job or promotion? The race to get hired is more competitive than ever with so many people just as qualified as you. Some people would agree that having a well-groomed look and carrying yourself with confidence can give you the extra edge. Demonstrating personal grooming shows that you care about your personal appearance. It communicates to the person you meet that they are important to you. When you display that the details of your grooming matters, it sends a message to others that you will pay close attention to the business details, and the needs of customers and clients. Always Be a polished poised professional.

5 professional tips for grooming-
    1. Bathe regularly, wash your body and your hair often.
    2. Trim your nails.
    3. Stand up straight.

4. Cleanse your face on a regular basis with facial soap.
5. Sleep at night.

5 grooming tips for the professional men-
1. Clean the hair off your ears and your neck.
2. Have your clothes tailored to fit the body and match your belt and your shoes.
3. Shine your shoes.
4. Cleanse your face on a regular basis with a facial soap.
5. Remember less is more when it comes to fragrance.

5 Grooming tips for the professional woman.
1. Dress for success don't let your other attribute take over your accomplishments.
2. Keep your nails clean short and neutral colored.
3. Go easy on perfume.
4. Dress professionally
5. Wear daytime make-up.

Posture-tips.

1. How to sit properly: Keep your feet on the floor or on the foot rest, if they don't reach the floor. Do not cross your legs. Ankle should be in front of your knees. Keep a small gap between the back of your knees in front of your seat. Your knees should be at or below the level of your hips. Adjust the backrest of your chair to support your low and mid back section or you sold your support. Relax your shoulders and keep four arms parallel. Avoid sitting in the same positions for long periods of time.

2. How to stand properly: Bury your weight primarily on the balls of your feet. Keep knee slight a bit. Let your feet align with shoulders/width apart. Let your arms hang naturally down the sides of your body. Your Shoulder should be pulled backwards stand straight and tall. Keep your head level and air lobes should be in line

3. Proper lying position: Find the correct mattress that is for you. Your comfort is important it will also reduce back pain. Sleep with the pillow. Special pillows are also made to help postural problems resulting from poor sleeping positions. Avoid sleeping on your stomach. Sleeping on your side or back helps with back pain. Place a pillow between your legs if you sleep on your side. If you sleep on your back keep a pillow under your knees.

4. Offensive hygiene to avoid: Picking teeth, nose, or ears. Sneezing, yelling without closing mouth, belching loudly, continuously rearranging here or close in the office desk areas. Even with your mouth open or making a noise while chewing your food. Remember you are well groomed, so stay Poised Polished and Professional.

Grooming Tips to Feel Confident

Nancy Hoogenboom

Poised, Polished, Professional is the title of this book, the question is how do we acquire these skills. Confidence is a key component, which we have already discussed. So, how does one become confident? Personal presence, the way one carries one's self demonstrates confidence. Attitude, personal style, posture, grooming, body language and clothing contribute to the impression of confidence. Before a person even speak a word he or she has been judged.

> *"You are your greatest asset. Put your time, effort and money into training, grooming, and encouraging your greatest asset."*
>
> ~ Tom Hopkins

As fair or unfair as it sounds, to judge and be judged, studies have found that people form an impression of another in the first seven seconds of interacting with that person. The way one presents oneself through speech and dress influences the opinions and perceptions of others. Knowing this information, taking time to present oneself well and authentically is extremely important.

According to research by Professor Emeritus Albert Mehrabian, professor at the University of California, Los Angeles, upon meeting someone for the first time face to face, a person forms an opinion that is 7 percent verbal, 38 percent vocal, and 55 percent visual. The majority (55 percent) of another's impression of another individual is shaped by the appearance. One's wardrobe plays an important role in appearance; but often personal grooming (and hygiene) may make the biggest impression. The little, not consciously noticed, aspects of one's self-presentation add up to an impression that is confident and poised in business and social situations.

Presenting oneself as refined and making others comfortable by considering our appearance is crucial. Poor grooming detracts from one's ability to build positive relationships with others. It inhabits our communication when a colleague is more concerned with our poor grooming than with what we have to say. Daily showering, brush teeth, and floss twice a day or more, keep teeth whitened and shampoo and condition hair often to keep it fresh and clean. Apply perfume, cologne or aftershave sparingly. Many people are allergic to perfumes and colognes. Grooming in pubic and work places are inappropriate. Co-workers, bosses, or clients don't want to see a colleague, employee, or business associate grooming. Grooming should take place before we leave our homes or in private (such as in a restroom or other personal space.)

> *"Fashion fades, only style remains the same."*
>
> *- Coco Chanel*

Grooming tips for women:

- **Hands:** clean and well groomed
- **Hair:** clean, neatly current style and appropriate for the occasion.
  Colored hair needs to be maintained.
- **Nails:** nail polish neatly manicured, no chip nail polish, no extreme colors
- Skin looking healthy and moisturized

- **Face Foundation:** Make up application should be moderate and enhance your natural features. If you have uneven elements to your skin such as dark spots or redness, you may wish to choose a foundation that evens out your skin tone. If your skin shows evidence of age, you may want to make use of a foundation that contains anti-aging elements. If you have clear, unblemished skin, a light foundation will still enhance your look because the anti-reflective quality of most foundations offset the sometimes harsh effects of the fluorescent lighting in many work environments.

- **Dental Hygiene:** Always maintain fresh breath, mints or mouthwash help avoid bad breath. Chewing gum is not appropriate at work.

- **Lipstick:** Blot lipstick if needed and check to make sure teeth are clear of lipstick. One's lipstick color should be relevant to one's work culture.
Eye Brows: Styled well
Tattoos: Depending on one's profession, cover tattoos if possible.

Faux Pas: This list is a reminder of things not to do in public, flossing, filing nails, painting nails, applying makeup, lip stick, applying lotion, brushing or combing hair in public, applying perfume in public places. If one happens to pass gas without warning, say, "excuse me" discreetly.

> *"Good grooming is integral and impeccable style is a must. If you don't look the part, no one will want to give you time or money."*
>
> ~Daymond John

Grooming tips for men:

- **Hair:** Keep hair well trimmed and neatly styled
- **Facial Hair:** Maintain a clean shaven look or trim any facial hair so that it is neat and clean looking
- **Eyebrows:** Neatly trim each eyebrow
- **Skin Care:** Use moisturizers and other skin care products regularly
- **Dental Hygiene:** Always maintain fresh breath, mints or mouthwash help avoid bad breath. Chewing gum is not appropriate at work.
- **Tattoos:** Depending on your profession, cover tattoos if possible
- **Nails:** Maintain Clean and manicured nails
- **Handkerchief:** Carry a Simple and clean handkerchief (keep a spare in your briefcase)

Faux Pas: This list is a reminder of things not to do in public, using toothpicks, grooming or touching your hair and facial hair. If you happen to pass gas without warning, say, "excuse me" discreetly.

Your first impression is extremely important in building long lasting business relations. Following these simple basic grooming tips is part of the overall professional appearance.

Correct Posture Boosts Confidence

Many times when I am at a business or social event people ask what my profession is. After I mention I am an etiquette trainer, people change their posture. If standing, they straighten to an upright, stiff-backed posture. If sitting in a relaxed position with elbows on the table, they pull their hands into their laps, place feet flat on the floor, and sit up so that their back does not touch the back of the chair. Their demeanor changes. Usually one person will ask, "How is my etiquette?" Since the number one rule in etiquette is not to correct others etiquette, I simply smile. Usually, the conversation about manners and etiquette continues and we discuss social and business etiquette.

How a person positions his or her body is important to non-verbal conversation. Open posture, that is, hands in one's lap or at one's side, a smile on one's face, and eyes focused on one's conversation partner communicates friendliness, attention, and positivity. Folding one's arms across one's chest and allowing one's eyes to travel around the room communicates non-attention, impatience, boredom, and general unfriendliness. Most of us can remember a time when we have been on the receiving end of both friendly and unfriendly posture. In a professional setting, one can do much to make a good impression by adopting an open, friendly posture. How we portray ourselves is often non-verbal.

When wanting to engage or connect with someone that may seem resistant, postural "mirroring" or echoing can be effective when done correctly. Mirroring someone makes them feel accepted and increases rapport. An example is to mirror their posture, seating position or gestures. This makes the person feel more comfortable and see themselves reflected in you. Use "mirroring" authentically and positively to increase goodwill between you.

Tips on Posture Etiquette:

- Always stand when being introduced, this helps establish a sense of presence.
- Note that a bent head and eyes turned down communicates distraction and inattention. Always keep your head up and eyes engaged with the person you are talking to.
- Men and Women should avoid crossing their legs in a meeting because it

can be distracting. Ladies, to sit proper, keep your knees and ankles together, ankles crossed if you prefer.
• Good posture will keep bones and joints in correct alignment and can help prevent fatigue. Poor posture is hard on the body and muscles can quickly tire if good posture is not maintained. Good posture will also give the impression of confidence while bad posture suggests disinterest.
• When having conversations, stand up straight; never lean against a wall.
• If one keeps one's chin always parallel to the floor, one will be well on the way to maintaining good posture.
• Practice proper posture to feel confident when walking, standing, sitting and entering a room.

One's posture reflects how one is feeling about oneself and business while you enter into your office, greet co-workers, arrive at a meeting, greeting a client for a lunch and much more. If you are feeling rushed and out of time, you are more likely to enter a room too rapidly and have your shoulders and back slump into a posture of defeat and self-censure. Regardless of your timeliness or lack of time, always "think tall." Upright posture communicates confidence and a readiness to engage. When you enter the room, make eye contact with those in the room. Make sure that your right hand is available to shake hands immediately on entering the room. Keep your back straight and reach your hand out so that it is parallel to the floor. For a business handshake, clasp your associate's hand "web to web" and shake twice firmly. A good handshake communicates that you are ready to engage positively with the situation.

Posture and deportment are equally important when you are engaged in a group activity. Recently I was in a business meeting. While seated at the opposite end from the speaker, I was able to observe the posture of those seated at the conference table. One gentleman's positive posture stood out. He was attentive to the speaker, sat up straight in his chair, and faced the speaker with his hands in his lap. He communicated engagement and respect. Others attending leaned on the table with their backs slouched, rested their elbows on the table with their hands under their chins, or leaned back in their chairs. Their body language communicated boredom and exhaustion.

Proper posture speaks volumes about you, whether your sitting, standing or walking. Whether one is at the water cooler or in a stand-up meeting, one's stance demonstrates one's mood and one's thoughts. Leaning against a wall presents a sloppy appearance and communicates disinterest, a lack of engagement, and tiredness. Standing up straight with squared shoulders, feet slightly apart, and hands at one's side shows strength, self-assurance, and readiness to engage.

Demonstrating how you care about the details in your personal appearance communicates the message that you will care about details in business. Taking the time to be well groomed and proper posture not only will make you feel confident, others will see the positive external characteristics and combined with a strong inside character equals respect. How you present yourself adds up to a huge difference, your overall polished personal brand equates to your success.

Poised Polished Professional

Developing the Essential, Professional Wardrobe

Nancy Hoogenboom

When you walk into a room, the first impression you make is created by your choice of dress and demeanor. How you feel in your clothing, shoes, accessories and the colors you choose make a difference in your confidence. Think about the time you wore your "power clothing and shoes", you could conquer the world. Now, remember when you wore something you wish you hadn't. Just the other day, I wore my "power dress" (3/4 sleeve royal blue sheath dress with a gold zipper accent on the front side) and "power boots" (black suede and patent leather ankle boot with a gold zipper running up the back, my husband bought me in London). I felt like a million bucks in that outfit and my demeanor equaled the feeling! On the flip side, many years ago I still remember speaking at an important meeting. My fashionable outfit with neutral-colored, leather shoes that were trendy, new and a size to small. My feet hurt so bad, I hardly made it thru the presentation. I learned a big lesson that day: a) make sure shoes fit properly and b) wear the shoes prior to the presentation.

> *"My philosophy is to look professional and approachable"*
>
> ~ Kate Spade

Constructing an essential wardrobe for your professional job is not as simple as you might think. First, you have to know the personality of your corporate office. Corporate offices can range from classic conservative to business casual. Know what your office expects. Daily, those in your office, from your boss to your peers, observe your soft skills, attire and posture. Dress for the position you want, not the one you have.

As you consider your wardrobe, solid colors are the most versatile for your essential basic wardrobe. Tailored clothing that fits well sets you apart. The style you choose for your body shape is important. Look for someone you admire with the same body shape as you and be inspired by their fashion.

Also look for someone who has the same challenges as you and who dresses well, note how that person camouflages those areas. Invest in essential wardrobe classics which suit you well.

The condition of the clothing that you wear makes as much of an impression as the clothes themselves. A designer suit with a button hanging by a thread will make a poor impression regardless of how neat and clean the rest of your appearance is. Take the time to make sure that your clothing is pressed and in good repair. Shine shoes, press shirts, steam skirts and dresses well ahead of time so that you are prepared for your interview, your day at the office, or your appointment with a client. Below are guidelines for your wardrobe. The best place to start shopping is your closet.

Women's Classic Conservative Wardrobe

A **suit** Jacket or blazer with pants or skirt to match is a must for a classic, conservative, professional look. The **jacket** should be sharp and sleek with clean lines. Slim, knee-length **skirts** with a back slit are a classic. **Pants** with a touch of flare at the hem offer a professional polished look. When shopping for a suit, pick up all the pieces that match so you may mix and match for a variety of looks. Choose neutral colors such as gray, black, tan, or navy and smart fabric choices include 100% wool, wool blend, lightweight stretch wool or polyester blend. Remember a power suit will vary from one profession to another; know the guidelines for your profession.

A properly accessorized **dress** allows one to walk out the door and into the boardroom with a minimum of fuss. In particular, the sheath dress offers a conservative and tailored look which you may dress up or down with blazer or sweater. Wrap dresses also provide a classic look. Find a brand that fits you well and highlights your best features.

Simple, solid-colored or white **blouses** and **tops** provide a good beginning to a basic wardrobe. Classic collar shirts lay well against a jacket or blazer. As you build your wardrobe, add print, striped, and floral blouses to present a personal sense of style or brand. Cotton, silk and polyester are good choices in blouse fabrics.

The Power of Accessories

"The most important accessory is your smile."

~Nancy Hoogenboom

Accessories make a statement, a belt, handbag, or scarf with a pop of color can add personal style to your wardrobe.

Below are the basic accessories for your essential wardrobe:

• **Handbag:** A professional, structured handbag will elevate your look. Look for a well-organized interior. Consider your profession and the items your bag will contain to determine the size of your handbag.

• **Briefcase or Tote Bag:** Select a professional style big enough to hold your business essentials. Some briefcases or totes have specific area for your laptop and smaller devices. Make sure the bag sits well (feet on the bottom of bag is a huge plus) and doesn't fall over when placed down. In addition, a zipper helps keep your items secure.

• **Shoes:** Classic pumps with a one-to-three-inch heel are considered the professional style. Closed-toe shoes are best for professional businesses. Keep away from open-toed shoes and sandals. Clean, polished shoes with no scuffs show you care about details in your appearance. Choose your shoes for comfort as much as for looks, especially if you are on your feet most of the day. Comfortable classic flats may be a better choice when you are on your feet most of the day. Black, navy and neutral colors work well for most wardrobe choices. If you would like to add some flare to your shoes, strappy pumps and boots may be a good choice for work once you know the culture of your office. Bows and a pop of color in your shoes can also add a sense personal style to your look.

• **Scarves:** Silk scarfs, whether in a solid or a print, add a pop of color to a professional appearance.

• **Belts:** Complement your outfit with a belt well chosen. One can make a dramatic, yet professionally appropriate, fashion statement with a wide belt or with a sophisticated slim belt for a pair of slacks.

• **_Jewelry:_** Jewelry can help set the tone for business interactions. If you are feeling a need to make a more personal connection with a client, it may be appropriate to wear a piece of jewelry that attracts attention and can be a conversation starter. If you feel you need to create a more professional atmosphere, clean, simple jewelry is best for a professional look.

• **_Watch:_** A timeless watch is worth the investment. Leather or metal band with classic dial details are best. Wearing a watch to look at the time (not your cell phone) is a small touch of manners that speaks volumes.

• **_Hosiery:_** Whether wearing tights or hose, a nude color is best for a finished look. Depending on your work environment, hosiery may be optional.

• **_Shapewear:_** For many, shapewear can add to a clean, polished look. Choose shapewear that fits and supports well.

• **_Cellphone:_** A mobile phone is part of your style. Keep your phone clean and use a classic cover.

As business casual becomes the modern business attire in many industries, a professional woman should have clothing appropriate to such attire in her wardrobe. Business casual overall can be less structured. Know your office rules for "business casual." A good rule to remember is to have three items to your outfit. When a more casual look is called for, combine a basic jacket or sweater with a print blouse, and a pencil or A-line skirt, a classic pair of pants, or a pair of casual Friday jeans. The third item "completes" the outfit. However, when you are wearing a dress, two items may complete the look.

Remember in business casual, anything that exposes to much skin (low tops and high hem lines) is inappropriate. If you ask yourself "is this **OK** to wear to work" most likely it's not a good idea.

Below are some other examples of business casual combinations:
- _Top, pant and sweater or jacket_
- _Blouse, skirt and sweater or blazer_
- _Dress and scarf_
- _Dress and Jacket or sweater_
- _Dress and bold necklace_

Men's Classic Conservative Wardrobe

Traditional *suits* now come in classic regular fit, trim fit (a medium-fitting suit with more of a shape) and extra-trim or slim fit (a fashion-forward suit that is narrow through the chest and has slightly higher armholes). The classic colors for suits include navy or charcoal. Select the suit that best fits your body type and the professional personality of your office and profession. Fit is key for suits. Have your suit professionally tailored by the store or from or a private tailor. **Suit jackets** should fit without gaping or wrinkling when buttoned and the length of the jacket should hit right in the middle of your hand when your arms are relaxed by your side. The sleeve length should reach the base of your hand. For a two-button suit jacket, always button the top button, and never button the bottom button. Three-button suit jacket, always button the middle button, sometimes button the top button, and never button the bottom button. Pants should "brake" at the top of your shoes. When wearing a suit for the first time, be sure that you have cut open the thread on the back vent and pockets of your jacket.

To accompany the suit, choose a solid or subtly printed **shirt**. Show a ½" of the cuff of your shirt sleeve below your suit jacket. Never wear a tie with a button down collar shirt. **Ties** should coordinate with the color of suit. For a sophisticated look, choose a solid or lightly patterned tie. Bold and themed ties are best left for casual days. The necktie should touch the top of your belt. To accessorize and to secure one's trousers, wear either a **belt** or **suspenders**, but never both. **Shoes** should be shined and in pristine shape. Understated socks are best for a finished tailored look. Black shoes are more business dress, brown are more casual and burgundy are fashionable.

To personalize your professional look, you may choose other accessories as well.

If you do, keep these simple guidelines in mind:

- **Watch:** Three elements; **Professionalism, Functionality,** and **Personal Style**, come into play when purchasing a watch or watches. A black leather strap with a classic face is the most professional choice, remember to match the leather color to your shoes and belt. A metal watch is practical and fashionable. Again, keep your metals the same as other accessories that are worn (wedding bands are the only exception to the rule).

- **Hats:** Pick the style and fit that is best for you. A fedora is a classic hat that looks good on most men. If you choose to wear a hat, remember that removing your hat is a sign of respect. Remove your hat when entering someone's home, at meal times, in houses of worship unless a head covering is required, at restaurants, schools, libraries or court houses. Whether indoors or outdoors, remove your hat and hold it against your chest when the national anthem is played. Hats may stay on at outdoor events, airports, hotel and office lobbies, on elevators and at athletic events.

- **Sunglasses:** Sunglasses are a practical and fashionable accessory. Make sure your shades are appropriate for your profession. When speaking with clients in business do not wear your sunglasses because being unable to see a person's eyes creates an unnecessary barrier between you and the client.

- **Briefcase:** A briefcase or day bag is part of your style, choose a bag that sits upright on the ground and is quality leather or fabric.

- **Cellphone:** A mobile phone is part of your style. Keep your phone clean and use a classic cover.

Business casual means dressing down your business attire, not dressing up casual wear. Knowing your industry's business attire will make dressing business casual easy. The range of business casual includes everything from suits with no tie, sport coats with jeans, shirts with pants, to t-shirt and pants. For a more casual look, color and prints are often worn with more casual shoes. Remember no matter how dressy or casual you dress, the proper fit and cleanliness of your clothing is essential.

> *"A man should look as if he had bought his clothes with intelligence, put them on with care, and then forgotten all about them."*
>
> ~HARDY AMIES

Personalizing within the boundaries of your profession makes you unique in your style.

Recently my client shared that the dress she receives the most compliments on is a deep burgundy wine, A-line sleeveless sheath dress with a 1940's large bow detail on the neck. She shared that it was purchased at a second-hand store. No matter what your budget is, shopping for the right style and color that best compliments you are important.

A senior management client has chosen to wear cowboy boots as his principal business shoe. The instep of cowboy boots is best for his posture. Classic, black, eel-skin boots are his basic boot choice, though he also wears other leathers choices and colors.

A perfect example of today's timeless fashion:

Kate Middleton, The Duchess of Cambridge, exudes a classic, chic, and timeless style. She adds a modern spin to a traditional, professional look. Dangling, pearl earrings replace classic, pearl studs. Her metal watch matches multiple outfits. Wedge-heeled shoes both add an element of personal style and allow her the stability needed for standing for long periods of time. Kate's genuine care for others permeates thru her posture and eye contact. Kate's inner beauty and kind confidence adds an important accessory to any outfit.

Cultivating your personal professional wardrobe while blending with your company's message and brand will positively impact business interactions. The small details add up to make you unique and confident as you present yourself in business.

Remember: when you think you look amazing; you show up amazing!

Poised Polished Professional

First Impression & Reputation Management

Leona Johnson

First t impressions are crucial In social situations, business settings, and when you are in customer service. If you give a bad first impression, they can cost you a job from prospective employers and you can lose confidence for the things you were excited about. First impressions can cost you business in many cases. An example of a bad first impression can be a person trying hard to please another or trying too hard to be memorable. This may turn off the person you are trying to impress. Never reveal your whole life history when you first meet a person. You never know what their lifestyle is about and problems he or she he may have. If you do too much talking about your own issues, you may cause an uncomfortable connection with the person you are talking to. Do not fill up space with a lot of talking because people do not usually follow along. Do not assume the first impressions are going so well that you trust the person you just met all too soon. Great social settings lead to people having great positive vibes. So, you reveal personal things to go along with the vibe, and the reality is that you can show immaturity to the person you are trying to impress. The first time you meet a person/customer/client, it will set the tone for many relationships with that person in the future. This behavior can set the tone for business relationships and personal relationships.

> *"You learn, just as you learn good manners, how to approach things with a certain amount of diplomacy.'*
>
> ~Robert MacNeil

However, you can certainly change your first impressions if you follow a few etiquette tips for future social situations.

1) When you go into any office to meet with clients, you have to be aware of others around you. Although your meeting is not with the secretary or

the office manager, you should always greet them with a warm smile and be friendly to everyone. When you are maintaining eye contact with others as you speak, it is a good first impression. You should always establish a great rapport with others; you will always be recognized and acknowledged. In some cases, employers ask employees what they thought about you.

2) When you greet someone for the first time, make sure you give a great impression by showing that you are confident within yourself. How you introduce yourself is very important. When you meet them, it should be with the firm handshake, displaying eye contact, greeting them by name, giving them a smile while you state your name and display a positive attitude; because people take notice of you. You should always thank them for meeting at the end of each meeting. This displays how important the meeting was to you.

3) If you want to give good impressions, conversation etiquette it is important. Try not to do all the talking when you're in a meeting. Try listening as much as you're talking. But taking your time to listen you will let the other person see that you have your full attention. The conversation may demonstrate that you're interested. Body language speaks volumes. It's the first thing a person will notice upon meeting you. If you are on your phone or looking at your phone when you first meet a person, you are sending a clear message that you're not interested in having a conversation with that person. When you are poised and standing straight with your shoulders back, arms to the side and have great eye contact, it will give indication that you are interested in the conversation or that you're ready to talk or to even do business. If you would like to impress a person during a business meeting, stay focused on that person at all times and maintain eye contact.

4) If you want to leave a good first impression, you must dress appropriately. This shows that you have respect for yourself, your business and customers. If you look appropriate, you look successful. Therefore, other people will have confidence in you. If you are not properly dressed or groomed, it is an indication that you don't care. When you are dressing in an appropriate manner, you will not distract clients or business colleagues from the message you're trying to give. If you are not sure about dress code for a meeting, stay safe and dress conservative.

Always make your first impression count, whether you are on a conference call or in a meeting. You have to start building relationships that last with businesses."First impressions" is actually a seven second window once you meet a person. When you're doing the interview process, you need to act fast in order to make a great first impression on the interviewer. If you want to give a good first impression during an interview, my etiquette tips would be for you to practice what you need to say about yourself and be prepared for follow-up questions. Dress appropriately, always learn about the organization or company through research, never over wear cologne or perfumes, limit your makeup and avoid appearing nervous; no negative body language, especially sweaty palms, that's one of the first signs. Most interviewers know within the first 30 seconds if you have a chance of getting hired. So put on your best first impression.

> *"If you don't want the nickname, don't live up to it."*
>
> —JENNIFER LEE CARRELL

During job interviews, some employers will try to impress the person they are interviewing to take the job by mentioning huge sign on bonuses or yearly packages that are very impressive. They will also talk about the company, its revenues and how it's growing to get a commitment from you. Then, once you're hired, they will ask what your first impression was of the company. First impressions are called that for many reasons. They are the foundation that employees start to build a relationship with managers & companies. The first impression will usually always lead to the last impression, depending on the types of experience in hand from day one. There is a common saying to it that we hear a lot. It goes, "You never get a second chance to impress a person."

In your personal life, a classic first impression is the introduction to a young lady's mother and/or father. In most cases, the boyfriend is terrified and he wants to know everything about the dad so that he can make the first best impression upon meeting him. Most guys are trying to impress press the dad first. Then, use charm on her mom to impress her; and most times it works. This is common. Most young guys want them to feel secure in knowing they have the best intentions for her and that's important to every parent. People dress differently when they are introduced to parents and that matters to them for good first impressions; and in most cases, you do not get a second chance. Make sure you give a proper introduction. Never look away, give the father a firm handshake and always thank them for having you. Your body language needs to display you being calm and relaxed. How you behave will also leave impressions on the girlfriend who brought you home to meet her parents. This could be the breaking point or making point.

First impressions when first dating someone is not like a job interview. You are not trying to create impressions on him or her, you are trying to figure them out to see if they are a fit for you. You should not try to impress a date. The problem is, you are being someone you are not and if the person would like to date you and have a more intimate relationship, you will be exposed once they know the real you. Be open, honest, charming and comfortable in your skin; because of this confidence your date will be attentive to you and your needs. Also, if you are trying to impress your date, do not pull out your mobile phone when it rings or vibrate unless it is an emergency. You do not want to lose thought or forget the conversation, especially on the first date. You will give the impression that you cannot have any of your own thoughts or conversations without getting thrown off by interruptions. Other impressive things about a person would be their choice of movies, books, music or attire; these things are a core of who we are. Your interest or hobbies reveals a lot about you. These are decision making things that provide emotional needs and it says a lot about who you are and it also depends on who you want to impress. When there are things that you can agree on that you like and you do the same, it could have a lasting impression on the person you intended on impressing. Always remember to make the right first impression.

Reputation Management

Reputation Management is removing negative content from businesses or individuals. Protecting and removing the information that has blocked your credibility as it relates to your business, job or individuals integrity. If your credibility is tested, it can ruin you from getting jobs, staying at a job or getting rehired for a job. It can also ruin your personal life and target your reputation to the point where you feel that there is no recovery for your image. When you are being searched online through websites and/or social media, these pages say a lot about who you are. Unfortunately, people judge your character from these results and it can drastically become harmful if they find negative content. Most people who are potential customers will search your business on web pages like they are a Job Recruiter looking for the best person or company for the job that they desire. It is important that you continue to check everything and all content that you put out on your web pages regularly.

You cannot ignore how you or your business appear in search results and the ratings you receive on other websites, especially if it appears on the top of search results. When you are working with big corporations, you have to be careful and accountable for your actions and how people perceive you, because it can cause the entire company's reputation to be on the line. One scandal can affect everything. Most companies already have reputation management on payroll just for these types of incidents. Sometimes people will sabotage this and find ways to demeanor your reputation. Be cautious and aware that there are people who target companies and individuals every day. These type of people make it their mission to damage and target others' reputation(s) for their own gain and satisfaction. If your reputation is targeted and damaged, you may find it hard to recover and you will need reputation management. At this point, you have to take full control and decide if you would like to hire someone to reevaluate ways to make a more positive impact to others. Reputation managers are a great way to start.

> *"It takes 20 years to build a reputation and five minutes to ruin it. If you think about that, you'll do things differently."*
>
> — WARREN BUFFETT

There are some Reputation Management Companies that will offer you a 100% success rate (or money back guarantee) for special technologies on removals. Reputation managers can charge anywhere from $3,000 to $10,000 just for monitoring your website for negative content. To remove your name for personal online negativity, it can be a little less but up to $6500, depending on whether or not they uncover others issues or remarks that has to be removed. During my research, I found that in some cases there are no magical ways to erase contact from the internet. There are things uploaded to the web that is impossible for you or a third party to remove without help from the administrator of that website where the content appears. It can be very difficult finding the right administrator for the site because of how most of the information is set up and according to the site and in most cases you have to provide lots of information before they even start helping. I found that even search engines like Google make it harder to remove content. Google has Cache results which means when you click a Cache link you can also review the content that was erased or removed. These results provide other ways for Management Reputation to use try removal techniques. Suppress techniques are used to create ways to make your online persona to tell a more positive story. In other words, they are pushing down the negative items so that when you search the internet, they will not appear on first pages of search result. This is a great way to keep negativity content in a long term strategy in case future negative content will arrive later.

    I had a friend who had her identity stolen. She was stopped at a routine traffic stop and was told she had a warrant. She was taken to jail and booked. She finally found out why she had a warrant. Stolen checks, the clerk said. She was mistakenly charged with a crime she did not commit. I can only imagine how humiliating that must have been. After spending 8 hours in jail, they finally released her because the video evidence showed it was not her according to a photo on file. Stolen identity is a growing illegal epidemic. Once she was released, she never thought about it nor did she want to be reminded. To clear her name, she hired a lawyer who discovered 6 months later that her mugshot and information about charge had not been removed and he had also pulled it up on several online websites. She was devastated and in her mind this was tragic. She worked as a High School Psychologist for over 10 years with children and this can damage her career. Her lawyer advised her that he would hire a reputation management lawyer to remove the file on each site as well as damage control with the police station where she was falsely arrested. It cost her (not including the original lawyer fees) a little over $3800.00 for him to remove all photos and information that can be publicly searched.

    She was one of the lucky ones. There are individuals and companies that do not act fast enough. They pay for removals from reputation management companies and later down the line, they are still paying to remove information. Make sure whichever company you use is a reputable company that you can trust. Search for other people who may have used the company and reach out to them for best results. Reputation Management is no easy task. These companies understand the importance of your brand, whether it's products, services or your individual reputation. Once they find out what's affecting your brand, their job is to effectively create a positive brand for you or your company. The types of content they control to come up with positive strategies or erased may include: mug shots, negative reviews, complaints, legal information, illegal information, defamatory contesting, media, articles, blog articles, revenge sites, bad publicity, photos, video, social media pages, web articles, blogs, web pages and more. These reputation management companies have a tough job. They undo negative damages that can be hard to regain.

Poised Polished Professional

Chapter V:
Attainment & Execution of Executive Presence

Models Attorney Neal White, Gina White, Actress
Photos courtesy of Teddy

Poised Polished Professional

Chapter V:
Attainment & Execution of Executive Presence

Karen Thomas

Once you have digested the information on the 3 Pillars it is now time to put them all together and use them on a daily basis. This practice should be a comfortable stance, not a struggle. Remember, these competencies are learned and if practiced daily in your professional AND personal life, will become second nature. Remember, you don't just wake up one day and decide you have executive presence. It is all learned, attained and maintained daily behaviors, most importantly with other in mind first and foremost.

Whenever I enter a room full of conference attendees or college workshop students, the one thing they immediately feel is the confidence I exude, the authority I garner with my posture, body language and the smile I offer to everyone I meet. This is the exact feeling that I want you to get and maintain once you have read, practiced and practiced some more, the content offered in this book. It may take some a matter of time and many career positions before it is attained and yet others will make these competencies their "Career Bible" so to speak, and project executive presence in a matter of no time at all. It all depends upon many factors, your career goals and exactly how much time you wish to devote to this matter. Again, there is no magic pill to take to attain this status, but with hard work, time and extreme confidence, you will do so.

> *"Be a yardstick of quality. Some people aren't used to an environment where excellence is expected.*
>
> *~Steve Jobs*

Poised Polished Professional

About the Compiler and Author
Karen A. Thomas

The Co-Authors:
Nancy Hoogenboom
Leona Johnson
Danielle Richardson
Carolyn Powery

Poised Polished Professional

Compiled & Authored by
Karen A. Thomas

Poised Polished Professional

Karen A. Thomas
Certified Etiquette Educator
Speaker, Author, Trainer
(860) 387-1282
Website: www.ctetiquette.com
email: ctetiquette@gmail.com
Twitter: https://twitter.com/Civilitysays
Instagram: https://www.instagram.com/ctetiquette
LinkedIn: https://www.linkedin.com/in/etiquetteessentialsct
Facebook: https://www.facebook.com/karen.scarfothomas

Your CT Etiquette Expert as seen on
ABC, NBC, FOX and CBS

Karen Thomas is known as the CT Etiquette Expert in Connecticut. Attracting individuals who value the importance of integrity, proper decorum and civility, Karen provides college lectures, workshops and corporate training, proven to increase self confidence, sales AND, leadership skills.

She is a monthly segment contributor/producer for 2 tv shows - CT Style on ABC-WTNH, in CT and Mass Appeal on NBC-WWLP, in MA. Karen is the go to etiquette expert for Star 99.9 FM radio - The Anna & Raven Show for Connoisseur Media, CT.

A well sought after speaker, known for her professionalism and humor, she speaks at conferences providing keynotes, breakouts and serves as a panelist. She has also author chapters for many books. Her chapter in the book "From the Soapbox to the Stage -- How to Use your Passion to Start a Speaking Business", by Bill Corbett outlines speaker etiquette and sought after etiquette advice.

Clientele includes, Aetna, Genworth Financial, New England Properties (Berkshire Hathaway New England Properties), Meeting Planners International as well as numerous corporations throughout the tri-state area.

Karen lectures at numerous colleges across the state of Connecticut including UCONN, Quinnipiac, University of New Haven and many more. Karen is the trainer to the UCONN Women's National Champion Basketball team and the UCONN football team as well.

Karen studied Business Administration in college and holds certification as an etiquette/civility educator trained in business etiquette, corporate leadership and educational advancement for youth. Karen resides in CT with her husband, Ken, 3 children, Robbie, Michaelanne and A.J. and her extremely well mannered dogs, Ruger and Jaxx.

What People are Saying..
"Karen offers an excellent presentation as well as the passion and knowledge and knows how to engage a crowd"
Steve Harvey, Harvey & Associates,

"I have worked with Karen at many events and am totally impressed with her expertise in the areas of etiquette and social protocol."
Mary Jones–WDRC show host

"Karen Thomas is regarded as a foremost authority in all areas of etiquette training and professional and personal development. She is known for consistently providing high-quality etiquette and protocol training programs and seminars that are focused and outcome oriented. Karen is dedicated to client satisfaction and organizational success, truly passionate about her work. I am honored and proud to be associated with Karen."
Sue Fox, Etiquette Survival, CA

Karen A. Thomas
Certified Etiquette Educator
Speaker, Author, Trainer

www.ctetiquette.com
email: ctetiquette@gmail.com
(860) 387-1282

Poised Polished Professional

THE EXPERTS' GUIDE TO EXECUTIVE PRESENCE

Co-Author
Nancy Hoogenboom

Nancy Hoogenboom
Founder and CEO of Daily Etiquette
562.201.0516, 866.452.5921
Website: www.DailyEtiquette.com
Email: Info@DailyEtiquette.com
Linkedin: www.linkedin.com/in/nancyhoogenboom
Facebook: www.facebook.com/DailyEtiquetteUSA
Instagram: Daily.Etiquette

Nancy Hoogenboom, Nancy Hoogenboom Is the founder and CEO of Daily Etiquette, Southern California School of Etiquette and Protocol. In addition to being a certified etiquette trainer, she is a speaker, author, consultant, and coach.

Nancy makes etiquette relevant for today's society in social media, personal interaction, and professional settings. Protocol and etiquette are always appropriate for business meetings.

By bringing the basics of etiquette into the day to day activities of our lives, Nancy is able to show new insights in communication with those in our lives.

Nancy lives in Southern California with her husband Neil. She enjoys her family, friends, and traveling. Also known as Fancy Nancy, her charismatic personality drives her flair for decorating and entertaining. Daily Etiquette looks forward to connecting with you for your professional and social speaking engagements.

Nancy Hoogenboom

Website: www.DailyEtiquette.com
Email: Info@DailyEtiquette.com
Linkedin: www.linkedin.com/in/nancyhoogenboom
Facebook: www.facebook.com/DailyEtiquetteUSA
Instagram: Daily.Etiquette

Poised Polished Professional

THE EXPERTS' GUIDE TO EXECUTIVE PRESENCE

Co-Author
Leona Johnson

Poised Polished Professional

Leona Johnson
CEO of All Manners Matter, llc.
412-607-3493
Email: Allmannersmatter@gmail.com.
Website: www.Allmannersmatter.com.
Facebook: www.facebook.com/AllMannersMatter
Instagram: www. Instagram.com/Allmannersmatter.
Linkedin: www. LinkedIn -Allmannersmatter

Leona Johnson Certified Etiquette Expert, Personal and Life skills Coach, Dating Strategists, Image&Branding Consultant and Certified Communicator Coach. She is the founder and CEO of **All-MannersMatter LLC**. located in Atlanta,Georgia.Her company showcases modern, Fun and engaging training that specializes in Professional Etiquette for all ages. Her programs teaches basic through advanced levels of Etiquette for integral development for both Business and individuals alike. Her company mission is to enhance one's holistic growth and develop ways to understand the importance of Etiquette and Civility. Her passion is Community Outreach. Making a conscious difference in the lives of others through Community Programs and Volunteering is rewarding. Leona has over 15 years of Volunteering in the local areas in Atlanta Ga .She is Cofounder of the **Women of Legacy** a nonprofit organization for Programs for empowering Women located in Stone Mountain , GA. She is a native of Pittsburgh PA, and a true Steelers fan that resides in Atlanta Georgia.

Leona is also available for Speaking Engagements.

Leona Johnson
All Manners Matter, llc.
Contact information: 412-607-3493
Email: Allmannersmatter@gmail.com.
Website: www.Allmannersmatter.com.
Facebook: www.facebook.com/AllMannersMatter
Instagram: www. Instagram.com/Allmannersmatter.
Linkedin: www. LinkedIn -Allmannersmatter

Poised Polished Professional

Co-Author
Danielle Richardson

Poised Polished Professional

Danielle Richardson, MBA
Inspire One Etiquette & Charm School

Email: info@inspireonetiquette.com
Website: www.inspireonetiquette.com
Facebook: www.facebook.com/inspireoneetiquette
Instagram: www.instagram.com/inspireoneetiquette
Linkedin: www.linkedin.com/in/daniellerichardson1

Danielle Richardson, MBA is the founder of Inspire One Etiquette & Charm School in Memphis, TN. Danielle has served in the capacity of coach and mentor in roles with several different organizations, both in her professional and volunteering life. Through various roles with the public school district, she recognized a critical need for etiquette and cultural exposure. She holds her Etiquette Consultant Certification from the prestigious American School of Protocol in Atlanta, GA and graduate of "The Finishing Touch" program at Minding Manners: International Etiquette & Protocol Academy of London, England, UK. Danielle is committed to pioneering a change and has a passion for teaching others how to positively influence the environment around them through modesty and grace.

Danielle is motivated by **1 Peter 4:10** which states;
"Each of you should use whatever gift you have received to serve others, as faithful stewards of God's grace in its various forms."

Social Media Links:
Email: info@inspireoneetiquette.com
Website: www.inspireoneetiquette.com
Facebook: www.facebook.com/inspireoneetiquette
Instagram: www.instagram.com/inspireoneetiquette
Linkedin: www.linkedin.com/in/daniellerichardson1

Poised Polished Professional

THE EXPERTS' GUIDE TO EXECUTIVE PRESENCE

Co-Author
Carolyn Powery

Poised Polished Professional

Carolyn Mercury Powery, MS
Prestige Etiquette and Image Consulting LLC
888-504-7716
Website: www.PrestigeEtiquetteandImage.com
or
www.carolynpowery.com
Email: PrestigeEtiquetteandImage@gmail.com
Social Media: LinkedIn: Carolyn Powery,
Instagram: @CarolynPowery
Facebook: Prestige Etiquette & Image Consulting@

Carolyn Powery is the CEO and Founder of Prestige Etiquette & Image Consulting LLC. She is a Certified Business Etiquette Consultant, Image and Personal Brand Coach for professionals, female entrepreneurs and young adults. She is passionate in helping her clients stand out and outclass the competition, convey a poised and polished persona, exude executive presence, and achieve success and excellence in their personal and professional lives.

She received her training and certification from The Etiquette Institute by Maria Everding. She is a member of both The Etiquette Institute (lifetime) and the National Association of Urban Etiquette Professionals. She has a Bachelor's degree from Bethune Cookman University and a Master's degree from Nova Southeastern University. Her etiquette institute has provided training nationally and trained international clientele.

She is the co-author of: Madam CEO: How to Think and Act Life a Chief Executive. Chapter Contribution - Preparing Young Ladies to be Professional Poised and Polished. Boys to Men: A Guide for African American Boys. Chapter Contribution - Becoming a Gentleman. She has been featured as an etiquette expert on media outlets including CBS Channel 12 News, NBC 6 In the Mix, and WPBF Channel 25. She has been quoted in magazine articles such as Southern Lady Magazine, XONecole, and The Boca Raton Observer.

Carolyn also brings a special perspective to her consultancy practice. As a former family counselor, she is able to positively impact young adults from a diverse array of backgrounds because she has worked extensively with teens and young adults for over three decades. Carolyn has been strategic in her program development for today's media-savvy youth and millennials, creating programs to assist them in achieving success. She is engaging, passionate personable, and knows how to relate to young adults in a method that makes them comfortable and receptive to her message.

Carolyn is available as a presenter and speaker at universities, businesses, corporations, public, and private school districts.

Carolyn Mercury Powery
Prestige Etiquette and Image Consulting LLC
Website: www.PrestigeEtiquetteandImage.com or www.carolynpowery.com
Email: PrestigeEtiquetteandImage@gmail.com
Telephone: 888-504-7716
Social Media: LinkedIn: Carolyn Powery, Instagram: @CarolynPowery
Facebook: Prestige Etiquette & Image Consulting

The Index

Gravitas-Pillar I
~Karen Thomas

Confidence
~Nancy Hoogenboom
Confidence comes from within
Increasing Your Self Confidence

Decisiveness
~Karen Thomas
Tips for Decisiveness in Business Situations

Integrity
~Danielle Richardson
Integrity – How to Stand?
Unwrapping Integrity for Executive Presence
1. Transitioning from the Inside Out
2. Perception
3. Enactment
From an Etiquette Expert Perspective

Vision
~Danielle Richardson
What is Vision?
Targeting Your Vision with a Purpose
1. Shift your paradigm
2. Paint a Picture
3. Speak like a Visionary
From Vision to Reality

Chapter III Pillar II-- Communication Conversation, Cell & Phone Etiquette

Communication
~Carolyn M. Powery
Communication Faux Pas
How to Communicate Effectively
The Three V's of Communication: Visual, Vocal, and Verbal
Tips to Consider when Developing your Communication Skills
Have Confidence
The Art of Listening
The Art of Articulation and Communication
Avoid Filler Words
Poise
Demeanor
Influence
Clarification
Common Executive Presence Questions
Ways to Communicate Executive Presence as a Woman
Tips for Improving Your Communication Skills
Conversation Etiquette - Message and Content
The Art of Small Talk
How important are listening skills when communicating?
Six Ways to Maximize Your Listening Skills
Use of Foreign Language around English Speakers
Cell Phone Etiquette
A professional greeting will create a professional image for your brand
Cell Phone Blunders
Telephone Etiquette

Conversation
~Karen Thomas
Cell & Phone Etiquette

THE INDEX

Netiquette & Paper Correspondence Netiquette
~CAROLYN M. POWERY
Cons of Social Media
Pros of Social Media Etiquette
The ABCDE's of Professional Netiquette
Appearance
Behavior
Communication
Social Media Faux Pas
Digital Footprint
Benefits of Social Media
Email Etiquette
Your Signature and Email Address
Voice Mail
Respond to Emails Within 24 Hours
Proper Protocol When Sending or Responding to Emails
Writing Professional Emails
Social Media Faux Pas
Digital Footprint
Benefits of Social Media
Email Etiquette
Your Signature and Email Address
Voice Mail
Respond to Emails Within 24 Hours
Proper Protocol When Sending or Responding to Emails
Writing Professional Emails
Chain Letters Emails in the Workplace
Sending Emails to a Group
Risks versus Benefits of Exposing Too Much Information
Proper Technology Etiquette in the Workplace
The Art of Paper Correspondence
Set Yourself Apart with a Thank You Note
Key Point Summary

The Essentials of Networking
~ Carolyn M. Powery
Executive Presence
How can you benefit from networking?
Networking Faux Pas
Tips to Network with Influence
Business Introduction Protocol When Introducing Others
Name Tag Etiquette
Ways to Remember Names
Proper Business Card Protocol
Business Card Exchange Etiquette
Successful Approach to Small Talk
How to Finesse Eating and Greeting at a Networking Event
The Power of Follow-Up

Body Language
~ Leona Johnson

Dealing With Difficult People
~ Leona Johnson

PART IV PILLAR 3- APPEARANCE
Grooming Posture
~ Leona Johnson
5 professional tips for grooming-
5 grooming tips for the professional men-
5 Grooming tips for the professional woman
Posture-tips.

Grooming Tips to Feel Confident
~ Nancy Hoogenboom
Grooming tips for women
Grooming tips for men
Correct Posture Boosts Confidence
Tips on Posture Etiquette

The Index

Developing the Essential, Professional Wardrobe
~Nancy Hoogenboom
Women's Classic Conservative Wardrobe
The Power of Accessories
Men's Classic Conservative Wardrobe

First impression & Reputation Management
~Leona Johnson
Reputation Management

Chapter V:

Attainment & Execution of Executive Presence
~Karen Thomas

THANK YOU

Thank you kindly for choosing our book. The journey of collaborating with other etiquette experts across the U.S. has been such a great experience both personally and professionally. Together we share a mutual respect for civility and etiquette that is evident in each chapter.

I'd like to personally thank each co-author for putting their trust in me directing this endeavor and collectively bringing a true experts guide to fruition

And finally, I thank you, the reader for allowing us to share our expertise in guiding your professional journey to the attainment of Executive Presence

Yours for a more civil society,

Karen A. Thomas
Certified Etiquette Educator
Speaker, Author, Trainer

www.ctetiquette.com
email: ctetiquette@gmail.com
(860) 387-1282

Poised Polished Professional